learn to

Relax

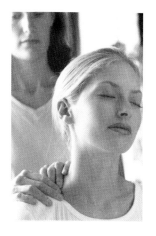

how to feel calmer
and more in control
of your life

Nicola Jenkins

p

This is a Parragon Book
First published in 2003

PARRAGON
Queen Street House
4 Queen Street
Bath BA1 1HE, UK

Produced by
THE BRIDGEWATER BOOK COMPANY LTD

Photography by
MIKE HEMSLEY AT WALTER GARDINER PHOTOGRAPHY

Photographic models:
ADAM CARNE, ANNE POWER

Hardback ISBN: 1-40542-296-3
Paperback ISBN 1-40542-298-X

Printed in China

contents

what happens to the body under stress

⋀ Stress release
Experts say that placing your head in your hands like this can help you find creative ways around a problem.

Recent statistics suggest that as much as 70 per cent of all visits to doctors involve conditions that are stress-related or that are made worse by stress. Stress is literally making us sick. If you are reading this book, then it is likely that you are already aware of some of the effects of stress on your own life or on the lives of those closest to you. You may be facing a serious physical disorder, recovering from a heart condition, having problems sleeping, or dealing with a range of emotional symptoms that are seriously affecting your ability to enjoy life.

A little bit of stress can be good for you. It makes you feel alert, able to concentrate effectively and perform to a high standard. With this, you often get a sense of euphoria, a natural high that arises because you have been able to meet a challenge successfully. That feeling of euphoria is addictive, however, which is why you may be tempted to continue at the pace you have set yourself, and why it can be a surprise when, after some time of performing at that level, your body begins to slow down and unpleasant side effects emerge.

Recognising that a problem exists is half the battle; the other half is committing to making changes in the way you do things so that you are able to relax. Commitment to relaxation means making changes, even if it involves letting go of long-standing habits, and keeping to the new habits once you have found what works for you. It is very easy to slip back into old habits when you are no longer focussing on your needs.

The following pages offer a range of simple, effective techniques that can help you to adjust your response to stress and aid relaxation. Before you try each and every suggestion, remember that you and your circumstances are special and unique – taking up a creative and expensive hobby isn't going to help you relax if the main reason you are under stress is because of severe financial burdens. Several small steps that can be integrated into your existing life are more likely to be effective, and will be easier to stick to.

In the 1920s, Dr Hans Seyle first described what has become known as the general adaptive response to stress. Seyle argued that there were three stages to stress:

∧ *Effects of stress*
Too much stress can cause physical, emotional and behavioural problems.

Stage 1 Alarm

This is the body's initial response to stress. During this stage, the body responds by initiating 'fight-or-flight' mechanisms.

Nerves send messages to the adrenal glands, telling them to release more adrenaline so that you are able to respond quickly. The immediate effect is that your blood volume and blood pressure rise, so that your heart, brain and skeletal muscles get the nutrients and oxygen they need. Your heart beats faster to keep the blood flowing to these critical organs, and blood-sugar levels increase so that you have the energy to fight or run away from whatever is causing the stress. The branching vessels in your lungs, the bronchioles, also dilate, allowing more air to enter the lungs, so that more oxygen becomes available to the body. Blood vessels in other areas of the body constrict to limit the supply of blood to parts not required for immediate survival.

Stage 2 Resistance

During the Resistance stage, the stressor has been around for some time and the body is adapting to its continuing presence. Long-term changes start to occur in the body to deal with the load added by the stressor. Instead of responding to stress by sending messages via the nervous system to the adrenal glands to release adrenaline, your body adapts to the long-term presence of the stressor by changing the levels of hormones in the body. This enables a slower, more easily controlled response.

Emotionally, you may have adapted somewhat to the new stressor, and it no longer produces the same level of response from you. You may have integrated any changes into your life to a certain degree, and feel that you are coping reasonably well. There may be certain physical symptoms developing to indicate that you aren't at your best; possibly you are aware of being frequently tired, or suffering from a range of other symptoms that appear mild when examined separately.

Stage 3 Exhaustion

At the Exhaustion stage, the body recognises that it is no longer able to cope with the continuing demands placed on it by the stressor or by a number of stressors. Resistance to stress and disease is severely reduced. Heart attacks and severe,

debilitating infections are more likely. Cortisol and other adrenal hormones have been present at high levels within the body for a long time. If cortisol levels remain high for extended periods, then any stored proteins within the body can be broken down, blood pressure will rise and more long-term changes can occur. This includes slower healing of cartilage and bone, loss of muscle tone, loss of bone protein and a lowered immune response.

At this stage, you may be experiencing more severe symptoms, telling you it is time to take action to reduce stress.

Cortisol

The key hormone involved in helping the body to adapt to long-term stress is cortisol. Normally it helps to keep your blood-sugar levels stable between meals and to maintain the volume of water in the blood vessels. However, when you are under a great deal of stress, you start to produce more cortisol. At high levels, cortisol will start to make sugar out of other substances – such as fat or protein, so that these can be used to provide alternative sources of energy for the body. This has a knock-on effect on other hormones with the result that you start to retain more water. For this reason some people experience bloating when under stress.

∧ *Fight-or-flight*
Raised adrenaline levels that prepare you to fight or run can increase aggression but also produce a sense of euphoria.

‹ *Tend-or-befriend*
Seeking out supportive friends or becoming more nurturing can be effective ways of combating stress.

Tend-or-befriend: Another kind of stress response

Recent research carried out by Dr Shelley Taylor, a psychologist at the University of California, Los Angeles, suggests that there is also another model for the way people adapt to stress. Dr Taylor refers to this as the 'tend-or-befriend' model, which appears to be more common in females than males. It refers to the tendency in humans (and other mammals) for females, when under stress, to nurture themselves and their young and to form strong alliances within a larger group.

This model does not exclude or replace the fight-or-flight instinct; Dr Taylor argues that it is probably just as long-standing: when humans still lived in caves, a female's aggression would have been more likely to be limited to the defence of herself and her children.

This response is due to the release of oxytocin – a hormone that enhances relaxation, reduces fear and promotes nurturing. When under stress, this hormone would help to ensure that a woman did not run away, but stayed to protect any children.

The tend-or-befriend model provides a biological reason why women in particular prefer to be with others, especially other women, when they are under stress, and why women are more likely to seek out social support mechanisms than men. We can learn from this that seeking nurture and support are effective aids to reducing stress, whether you are male or female.

signs and symptoms of stress

Each one of us experiences stress in a completely personal way and exhibits the symptoms of stress in a unique fashion. No matter how stressed you are, it is highly unlikely that you will be showing all the physical, emotional and behavioural symptoms of stress. Instead you will show patterns of symptoms that vary according to how badly stressed you are. Learning to recognise your personal early signs of stress, and taking effective steps to relax at that point, can head off the more severe symptoms you might face later on.

∧ *Exercise*
Taking regular exercise is a great way of calming the mind, which is a key step in learning to relax.

PHYSICAL
SYMPTOMS

Increased alertness (initially)

Increased heart rate

Increased blood pressure

Muscle tension (especially in the upper back, neck, chest and jaw)

Increased headaches and migraines

Suppressed immune system

Raised blood-sugar levels

Increased metabolic rate

Lowered blood supply to extremities, so poor circulation gets worse

Lowered blood supply to skin means increased likelihood of skin complaints

Lowered absorption of nutrients in bowel

Less movement in digestive system means increased risk of constipation and IBS symptoms

Bowel disorders increase, including diarrhoea, constipation, nausea, vomiting and ulcers

Kidneys retain sodium and water, higher risk of oedema and bloating

Disturbed sleep or insomnia

Breathing becomes faster and more shallow

Dry mouth

Lowered resistance to viruses (such as the common cold, cold sores or similar)

Lowered libido or impotence

Lowered sperm count

Menstrual cycle disrupted

Fertility decreased in both men and women

∨ *Double trouble*
Stress can make you withdraw from others and stop you wanting to communicate with loved ones.

EMOTIONAL SYMPTOMS

Increased irritability

Increased anger or hostility

Depression

Jealousy

Restlessness

Anxiety

Inability to make decisions

Withdrawing from others

Avoiding social events

Lack of interest in others

Tearfulness

Over-critical of self or others

Tendency to put oneself down

Inability to see positive aspects of one's situation

Obsessive focus on an event, situation or person, unable to be distracted from the problem area

➤ Signs of stress
Signs that you are under too much stress range from restlessness and anxiety to sexual disinterest and comfort eating.

▼ Bottling it up
A popular source of comfort, alcohol actually increases the physical stress on your body and could send physical symptoms spiralling out of control.

BEHAVIOURAL SYMPTOMS

Increased smoking

Increased alcohol use

Increased use of recreational drugs

Over-eating or comfort-eating

Under-eating or skipping meals (loss of appetite)

Changed eating habits (or tastes in food)

Lethargy

Becoming more accident-prone

Compulsive behavioural patterns (such as a sudden urge to wash hands, etc)

Sexual disinterest

Speech difficulties, including stuttering, stammering

Displacement activities to avoid urgent tasks, for instance, excessive television viewing

◀ Create order
Prioritizing tasks and setting deadlines helps develop security, predictability and calm.

Severe Stress

You are more likely to experience severe side effects of stress if you:

Set yourself extremely high standards

Find it difficult to say 'no'

Feel you are constantly in danger of letting yourself or others down

Lose sight of the difference between minor and major problems and overreact to minor ones

Become unable to prioritize between minor and major or urgent and non-urgent tasks

Avoid the major or urgent tasks, spending too much time on less demanding activities

Get impatient when things don't happen when you want them to

Insist that the way you do things is the right or best way

Feel guilty that you 'should' or 'ought' to be doing more

Are unable or unwilling to delegate tasks or ask for help

Regularly double-book yourself for events etc.

Taking action to combat stress

Research into people's physical and emotional responses to stress has led the experts to agree that stressors that are unpredictable and uncontrollable have a significantly worse effect on the individual than those situations where they can exert some control. Repeated exposure to these unexpected events leads to long-term debilitating effects, including severe depression. To promote relaxation, you need to do the following:

REDUCE STRESS. Avoid the source, or take significant action to change how it affects you.

CHANGE YOUR REACTION TO STRESS. Develop coping strategies to deal with stress.

FIND AN OUTLET FOR FRUSTRATION. Don't bottle it up, but find a harmless way of releasing your tension.

ENHANCE YOUR PERSONAL SENSE OF CONTROL. Develop security or predictability in other aspects of your life.

ten steps
to relaxation

The following steps can help you to reduce stress, change your response to it or regain a sense of control in your life. Finding effective outlets for your frustration needs consideration. Take time to think about activities that excite or inspire you. The outlet you choose needs to be something that you are going to really enjoy; finding time to relax is difficult enough without using that time to punish yourself.

∧ Healing touch
A shoulder and neck massage can help to reduce some of the physical symptoms of stress.

Catch your breath

Monitoring your breathing is one of the easiest and most effective ways to achieve a deep sense of relaxation. When you are under stress, it is common to start to take faster and more shallow breaths. To relax, you need to reverse the process:

BREATHE FROM YOUR DIAPHRAGM. This allows your lungs to fully inflate, which means you will get more oxygen to your brain and body whilst calming the mind. If you are breathing from your diaphragm, your abdomen will also move as you inhale and exhale. Try breathing in this fashion for ten slow inhalations, pausing before slowly exhaling. At the end of this time, you should feel very relaxed, if not euphoric.

Burn frankincense

This essential oil actively encourages you to breathe more deeply, as well as opening the airways in the lungs. Used for centuries in churches, it helps to create a meditative atmosphere and aids deep breathing and a calm approach to crises.

COUNT TO TEN. This old favourite really works, allowing you time to calm down before responding in times of crisis. Rather than over-reacting to a new stressor, sit down, count to ten slowly, taking a few deep breaths, then proceed, only moving slower than you did before.

DON'T RUSH. Make every effort to give yourself enough time to complete your tasks and get to where you need to be without becoming panicked. Soothing music played en route will also help you to relax.

USE PUBLIC TRANSPORT. If the transport infrastructure is suitable for your journey you have a chance to sit down on the train or bus. Then you can catch up on tasks whilst travelling or relax with a book or gentle music.

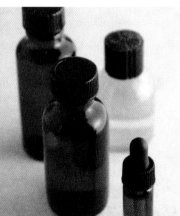

≪ *Breathe!*
Essential oils that encourage deep, relaxed breathing include frankincense, cedarwood, lavender, sandalwood, rosewood, marjoram and benzoin.

2 Create a haven

A haven can be found or built anywhere. It should be a space where you feel totally comfortable and secure, where you can control the sights, sounds and textures, and where you also have some control over who attracts your attention. In your haven you can relax and recuperate from the daily grind.

SELECT CALM COLOURS. Generally, lighter, softer colours and pastels are deemed to be more relaxing than strong, vibrant colours. Soft mauves, pinks, blues and greens all help to calm the mind, relax the body and reduce anger or frustration. Strong yellows, oranges and reds tend to stimulate the body and mind, and should be avoided in large amounts in areas where you seek relaxation.

USE SOUND TO CHANGE THE ATMOSPHERE. Tibetan chimes, Balinese bells, singing bowls and similar space-cleansing agents are excellent for altering the atmosphere of your room. If your haven doubles as your living room, use these when you first enter the home at the end of the day, or if people have been arguing.

ADD PLANTS OR OTHER ASPECTS OF NATURE. As well as bringing harmony to your surroundings by adding the colour green, plants take in carbon dioxide and release oxygen during respiration. Increased oxygen helps you to think more clearly.

Colours for calmness

If you are already experiencing high blood pressure, reducing the amounts of stronger colours in areas of your life outside the home can also have a beneficial effect. Why not replace red folders and desk equipment with blue ones?

Reduce noise levels

Try working in a quiet room, lowering the ringer tone on the telephone, or screening calls for part of the day. If you work in an open-plan environment or are hot desking, try using a personal stereo or earplugs to reduce the effect of stressful distractions. At home, try muting the television, telephone and radio output. Invest in double glazing to cut out street noise. Alter the kind of music you listen to. Choose music that has a slow rhythm and makes you feel relaxed and uplifted.

Play classical music

Classical music, especially if it does not involve singing, has long been held to be calming. Recent reports indicate that Mozart's music in particular is very effective at reducing stress and anxiety, and aiding study.

Your haven
Create your own haven with calm colours, comfortable furnishings, peaceful sounds and elements from nature.

GET A PET. Research indicates that time spent stroking or petting an animal helps to reduce blood pressure and heart rate.

CHANGE THE LIGHTING. Bright and overhead lights help to stimulate the mind and keep it alert. To aid relaxation, use low lighting in your haven. Put low-wattage bulbs in lamps, dim overhead lamps or light candles instead.

REDUCE OR GET RID OF CLUTTER. Remove any clutter from the space you have designated as your haven, or at least stack it neatly out of sight. If your clutter involves paperwork and similar activities, set aside time to deal with it.

USE COMFORTABLE FURNISHINGS. Any furnishings in your haven need to be completely relaxing. Change the decor if there is anything that you don't like or that upsets you.

GET AN IONIZER. These electrical appliances are now readily available and help to reduce the levels of chemical pollutants, pollen, dust and dirt to manageable levels within a room. People using ionizers often report improved sleep and a more relaxed state of mind.

AIR THE ROOM REGULARLY. Airing your haven helps to increase the amount of oxygen in the air. It removes stale odours and enhances the sense of calm and relaxation within.

USE FRAGRANCES. Air fresheners or essential oils in a vaporizer can add a calming touch to your haven. Use up to ten drops in a vaporizer for a lasting effect.

MAINTAIN THE ROOM TEMPERATURE. Your haven should be at a comfortable temperature. Whilst finances might suggest that you need to limit the amount of heating you use, remember that feeling cold for a long time increases stress and puts pressure on your immune system, making you more vulnerable to infections.

3 Make time to take time

The most common problem associated with being under stress is a lack of time to do what you want to do. Yet there are often small habits that we have that, when examined or altered, can save us the time we need in order to get some breathing space.

KEEP A DIARY FOR TWO WEEKS. Be as honest as you can be about everything you do. This will show when you are most and least effective. To make the diary even more insightful, give an indication as to how you felt at the time – stressed, relaxed, worried, happy, sad, etc.

HANDLE EACH PIECE OF PAPER ONLY ONCE. Unanswered letters and unpaid bills can easily mount up if they are allowed to. See how long it takes you to deal with a problem by making a pencil mark in one corner of the piece of paper each time you touch it. Rather than avoiding the paperwork, make the effort to handle each item only once, even if this means you leave all letters and bills to be dealt with once a week.

RATIONALISE YOUR SHOPPING. Frequent trips to the supermarket can be stressful and a waste of time. Try going less often but picking up everything you need for a week or two. Alternatively, order your groceries over the internet. Even if the supermarket charges a delivery fee, think of it as an investment in your sanity.

Make a list

Writing lists of things to do is extremely helpful if you worry that you might forget something important. You can also use these lists to help you to prioritize your tasks, so that the most important things get done first.

DELEGATE. There are usually many tasks in the home and workplace that may be open to delegation. Even if the person you delegate them to doesn't do the tasks the same way as you, allowing the individual to try helps develop his or her own skills and eases the pressure off you. If you are badly overworked and feel you have no one to support you at work, you may want to discuss this issue with your employer to see if any help is available.

USE AN ANSWERPHONE. Even if you are home, screen your telephone calls for at least part of the day, for instance during meal times, and save returning those calls for a time when you are able to concentrate on the person phoning.

REWARD YOURSELF. Draw up a list of things you would like to do if you had the time and treat yourself to one of them each time you tackle a major or urgent task you know you have been avoiding.

USE A DIARY OR CALENDAR. Get into the habit of recording all appointments or social events in one place. This will help you to co-ordinate any events with partners or other household members as well as ensuring that you don't double-book yourself. Remember to timetable in your relaxation rewards!

COMMIT TO YOURSELF. Once you have found the time and space in which to relax, don't let anyone else put anything in that time. You have worked for the time off, you have earned it, now you need to go and enjoy it! Do not allow yourself to feel guilty or to use this time to carry out a chore. Taking time off, even if it is only half an hour to have a soak in the bath, will leave you relaxed and refreshed and better able to cope with existing problems.

LIFE STAGE STRESSORS INCLUDE

Moving house

Change or loss of relationship

Parents' or children's change or loss of relationship

Redundancy or loss of job

Change of job

Financial concerns

Pregnancy

Physical illness

Examinations

Family members moving or leaving home

Change of sleeping habits

Bereavement

Personal injury

Bullying or harassment at work or school

∨ *Shopping*
Save time and effort by shopping online when it suits your schedule.

> *On demand*
Screening calls lets you control how and when you deal with telephone interruptions.

4 Calm the mind

Mental exercises, however simple, make the greatest difference in helping you to relax. Without calming the mind, physical relaxation is virtually impossible. Even if you keep meditations or visualization activities to five minutes a day, their effects are very long lasting.

MEDITATION. One of the most effective methods of relaxation, meditation helps you to focus and clear your mind, reducing the effect of whatever problems are worrying you. It also requires next to no equipment. To prepare for meditation, simply select a comfortable place to sit or lie down, where your back is straight and your limbs are arranged comfortably, and where you are not going to be disturbed by distractions or changes in temperature. Close your eyes and counting the inhalations focus on your breathing. Concentrate on slowing it down. Allow your mind to drift, even if it goes back to the problems that are worrying you. Don't worry if you find it difficult to meditate for more than five minutes at the start; this is normal. If you persevere you will soon see results.

WALKING MEDITATION. If you find it difficult to sit still to meditate, try a walking meditation. This can be done anywhere, either in your garden, in your home or out in nature. It is important that you walk slowly

Affirmations

These are short sentences that you repeat whenever positive thinking is required. As well as helping you to put a positive spin on any situation that is worrying you, these sentences can be used to help you to relax if you say them either out loud or to yourself every time you are thinking about an issue that worries you. Try 'Creative solutions and wonderful opportunities present themselves to me constantly', for example. Remember, the more you repeat them, the more effective they become.

through the area you have chosen, allowing your mind to clear. Watch the pace at which you walk; you are more likely to speed up when thinking of a problem. When this happens, stop, look around you and stand still until you are able to release the problem, then walk on, only more slowly.

CREATIVE VISUALIZATION. This can be done as part of a meditation, or at any other time. Think of it as daydreaming with a purpose. For this exercise you need to imagine yourself in a particularly calm and serene environment, either a place you know or somewhere you would like to be – a hammock on the beach, perhaps? Picture yourself there as clearly as you can. As you become more comfortable with the visualization process, you can introduce new elements to it; why not picture a waiter arriving at your hammock not only with a tropical drink, but also with something that represents a good working solution to whatever problem you are facing?

EMOTIONAL STRESS RELEASE.
Kinesiologists refer to a particular area of your forehead as the emotional stress release point; this is where you place your hand automatically if you rest your head on it. Simply resting your head in this position for a few seconds can help to calm you down and is also a very effective way of encouraging you to think laterally – and find those creative solutions.

EXERCISE. Any form of physical activity can be a great way of calming the mind and providing a positive outlet for releasing any lingering frustration or rage. Choose an activity that you enjoy and that will take your

mind off your worries. The most effective exercises for calming the mind are those that require you to concentrate on your breathing whilst working (such as swimming, long-distance running or yoga) or that are complex enough that you need to focus your mind on your actions whilst working (try any aerobics class or martial art, horse-riding, sailing or windsurfing). For best effects, pick an activity that takes place outside, as the fresh air can make a big difference.

∨ *Walking tall*
Wherever you go, walk with your head up; you're guaranteed a better view and a sunnier disposition than if you focus only on your feet.

< *Visualization*
Concentrate on visualizing your personal version of serenity.

<< *Focus*
Martial arts, such as Tai Chi or Chi Qong, can help you achieve clarity of mind.

5 Massage for partners

Massage is an extremely effective way of aiding relaxation as well as improving communication between partners if stress or conflicting demands have contributed to a loss of intimacy. If time allows, treat yourselves to a warm, relaxing bath before starting the massage. Not only will this enhance the effects of the massage, but it will also soften up the muscles a bit before you work on them, making the treatment more effective.

Don't be surprised if there is an urge to fall asleep after the treatment. This means you are doing a good job! Regular massage, even if it is only a ten-minute treatment three times a week, can make a huge difference to your approach to life and to each other. The following short treatment for the back concentrates on those areas prone to stress-related muscular aches and pains.

∨ *effleurage*

BACK MASSAGE. To encourage deep relaxation during the massage, make sure that your partner is lying comfortably, either on the floor or on the bed. In either case, you will need to kneel beside him or her to carry out the treatment.

Gently warm any oil or lotion that you will be using during the treatment before applying it – try putting the bottle of oil in a bowl of warm water beforehand.

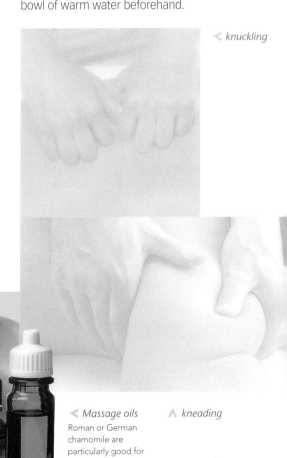

≺ *knuckling*

≺ *Massage oils*
Roman or German chamomile are particularly good for muscle relaxation.

∧ *kneading*

EFFLEURAGE. Apply the oil in smooth, flowing strokes, working from the hips up to the shoulders and neck, then gliding down the sides of the body back to the hips to repeat. Keep this stroke rhythmic, slow and smooth. Repeat until you can feel the skin and muscles warming and relaxing beneath your hands. Repeat for smaller areas as well, concentrating on the hips and waist area, the mid-back and then the shoulders.

KNEADING TO THE BACK. This movement involves you picking up the flesh with one hand then passing it to the other in a side to side movement. Work your way up one side of the body then down the other, spending more time on the shoulders, where most people hold a lot of tension. Remember to keep the movements slow and rhythmic. The slower you go, the more relaxing the movement is for the person you are treating.

▽ petrissage

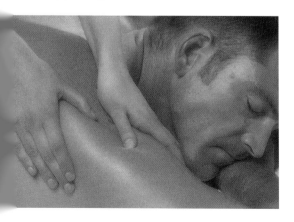

KNUCKLING. This uses the first joint of the fingers to work deeper into tight muscles and is particularly useful over the shoulders and hips. Place your knuckles on your partner's back, keeping your wrists straight (so that you can lean in with your body weight and press deeper), and rotate your hands from the wrists. This movement is very relaxing if done slowly and is also very effective if your partner has extremely tense muscles. It also saves your hands and wrists if you find the massage painful to perform.

PETRISSAGE. Use your thumbs to make small, grinding circles about the size of a ten-pence piece. This movement is great for releasing particularly tight muscles and feels wonderful when done very slowly. Use this movement around the shoulder blade and along the tight bands of muscle often found on either side of the spine. After you have tried the small circles and repeated the movement at least three times, press just as hard and run your thumbs along the area you have just worked on.

Knead the neck with one hand, then follow up with small petrissage movements just below the base of the skull.

Repeat the kneading and then the smooth flowing effleurage strokes. As you are about to finish the massage, gradually make your strokes slower and lighter until you are just stroking your partner very gently.

6 Try natural remedies for stress

Alternative therapies offer a huge range of treatments and remedies for stress and are generally extremely effective at aiding relaxation. Each person has a unique response to treatment, so finding the best method for you can be a great experiment. Speak to friends and relatives in the first instance; often they will be able to recommend a therapist. Most therapies also offer ways that can help you to relax in-between treatments, some of which are listed below:

▲ Homeopathy
Most remedies work best if you avoid tea, coffee or strong peppermint sweets. Switch to non-minty flavours of toothpaste too.

FLOWER REMEDIES Bach Flower remedies are available in most health food shops and chemists and provide emotional support in times of trouble. To use them, you just take a few drops either in a glass of water or straight on to your tongue several times a day.

Try Centaury if you find you are taking on too much, Elm if you find responsibility overwhelming, Hornbeam if you are aware that you are delaying taking action, Impatiens if you are impatient or frustrated, Oak or Olive if you are exhausted and have to keep going. Don't forget the blended Rescue Remedy for severe shock, exam stress or mental anguish.

Hand reflexology

Any form of reflexology is extremely good for reducing stress and aiding relaxation. Hand reflexology allows you to treat yourself at any time during the day, especially when you are feeling particularly stressed. The solar plexus point – in the centre of your palm, directly below your middle finger – is the place to work if you are feeling very upset. This is often sensitive to touch when you are very stressed. Rotate your thumb over the spot, pressing down in small circles. Press as hard as you can comfortably do.

HOMEOPATHY There is a wide variety of homeopathic remedies that ease some of the symptoms of stress. Gelsemium is useful if you feel anxious about forthcoming exams, interviews or presentations. Lachesis helps if you are suffering from mental or physical exhaustion as a result of working too hard. Lycopodium aids those experiencing a lack of self-confidence and mood swings. Nat. mur is useful for those feeling tearful or over-sensitive who also experience water retention and migraines as a result of stress. Staphysagria is useful when your response to stress includes feelings of resentment, anger or humiliation. If you want to find a blend that is carefully chosen to meet your personal needs, contact a professional homeopath.

Lavender
Use lavender to make sedating sachets to fragrance bedlinens.

Flower remedies
Take these in a glass of water or directly on the tongue.

Reflexology
Work the solar plexus point in the centre of the palm to subtly reduce the effects of stress.

Blissful bathing
Warm baths are more relaxing than hot ones. Add sea salt, sodium bicarbonate or essential oils to reduce anxiety.

ESSENTIAL OILS FOR RELAXATION AND TO REDUCE STRESS

Benzoin	Melissa
Bergamot	Neroli
Cedarwood	Orange
Clary Sage	Palmarosa
Coriander	Patchouli
Frankincense	Petitgrain
Geranium	Roman
German	chamomile
chamomile	Rose
Ginger	Rosewood
Grapefruit	Sandalwood
Jasmine	Tangerine
Lavender	Vetiver
Lemon	Yarrow
Marjoram	Ylang ylang
May chang	

AROMATHERAPY Essential oils used in vaporizers or in the bath aid relaxation and help to still the mind during meditation. For shock, nervous tension or anxiety, try a few drops of Neroli on a tissue, which you can sniff when you feel most unhappy, or try a combination of the essential oils suggested here. You can work with 10–15 drops of essential oil in a vaporizer, a maximum of 6 drops of essential oil in a full bath or 8 drops in 20 ml of a carrier oil if you are applying the essential oils for massage. If the person receiving the bath or the massage is pregnant or breastfeeding, under 12 years of age, has sensitive skin or a serious medical condition, please contact an aromatherapist before applying essential oils to the skin.

7 Change how you respond

The way we perceive and respond to a stressor is often what makes the situation harder to deal with. Your existing responses may mean that you are easily talked into doing things that you don't have the time or inclination to do. These suggestions will help you to manage your time.

ACTIVE LISTENING. These simple techniques help you to make sure that you are completely focussed on the person speaking. Check that you understand what they are saying, and ensure that they have had a chance to express themselves clearly. This kind of focussed attention helps you to avoid any misunderstandings, to build

▼ Listening skills
Focus, eye contact and relevant questions all help to create effective communication.

Pause for thought

Aim to take time out to consider any problem and your response to it before reacting. With the one exception of physical danger to yourself or others, most 'challenges' will benefit from some time to think before you tackle them. The same goes with people. If you are asked to take on a job or a responsibility that you are unsure about, ask for a little time to get back to the person with an answer, and stick to what you say.

deeper relationships or mend those in which communication is suffering. Make eye contact whilst the person is speaking. Stop what you are doing to listen to them whilst they are speaking, let them speak without interruption and only ask questions that relate to the topic under discussion and that are open-ended (so they have to answer with more than a 'yes' or 'no'). Then paraphrase what the person said to show that you have understood it properly.

THE BROKEN RECORD. Often people don't hear what you are saying to them if you are trying to say 'no' without causing offence. The broken record technique requires you to find an inoffensive sentence that makes it clear that you are unable to do what they ask. You repeat it without variation until the

> *Broken record*
This technique helps establish your boundaries, encourages others to delegate appropriately and set reasonable tasks. It can also show how and when you are able to provide support outside your remit.

< *A positive spin*
Using more positive language to describe things leaves you feeling more secure in your ability to cope. Negativity has the opposite effect.

< *Take time*
Before responding, clarify deadlines and the nature of the task. Then prioritize accordingly to avoid senseless rushing.

person you are speaking to registers what you are saying. For instance, if your boss unexpectedly wants you to stay at work very late one evening, say 'I have to leave work at 5.30 tonight'. No explanations, no excuses, simply state your boundaries.

CHANGE THE WORDS. Your body and mind believe everything you say. Using more positive words to describe your personal situation and whatever issues you are facing is effective not only in raising your self-esteem, but also in helping you to feel more confident of your success and more relaxed about the situation. Problems become 'challenges' and chaos becomes 'opportunities for change'. Focus your mind on seeking solutions rather than on restating the problem.

DON'T RUSH YOUR RESPONSE. Asking people to clarify the nature of the task, the deadlines and what their expectations are can help you both to establish shared priorities. It can also help you to maintain control over your own schedule.

8 Alter your work habits

Taking a detailed look at how you work as well as the kind of stress that work adds to your life can make a huge difference, especially if the problem lies with the amount of unpredictable or uncontrollable stress involved in your day-to-day life. Try some of the following ideas to bring a more relaxed approach to your working life:

∨ Home work
Try working at home when you need extended quiet to concentrate.

> Public transport
Whilst frequently crowded, using buses and trains lets you catch up on reading and planning your day.

> Clean desk
Tidying your workstation at the end of the day encourages a clear mind in the morning.

< Repetitive strain
Check that your workstation is appropriately organized to avoid physical discomfort at work.

CONSIDER THE JOURNEY TO WORK.
If extensive driving is making you unhappy, re-evaluate how you travel to work as well as the length of time it takes. One option may be switching to public transport and using the time gained to catch up on your reading or correspondence. Or, if possible, you could walk or cycle all or part of the way.

NEGOTIATE WORKING AT HOME. If your work requires undisturbed periods for creative thinking, working from home on a regular basis can be extremely effective.

WRITE LISTS OF THINGS TO DO. This will help you prioritize your tasks so that important things get done when they are required.

OPERATE A CLEAN DESK POLICY. No matter how busy you are, spend five minutes at the end of the day tidying your work to help put you in a more relaxed frame of mind when you arrive the following morning.

CONSIDER DOWNSHIFTING. The decision to change your career for one with either fewer financial benefits or in a less

< *Time out*
You can work more effectively if you take regular short breaks, avoid frequent overtime and take time off to recover when you are sick.

prestigious setting can bring about abrupt changes in your stress levels. People often downshift because of the improved quality of life that will accompany a move to a quieter area, or because a job switch will allow them more free time in which to relax.

TAKE REGULAR BREAKS. Taking five minutes every hour just to get up and stretch your legs can make a big difference. Even if deadlines are looming, a short break can help you to return to your task revitalized.

TRY TO AVOID WORKING OVERTIME.
Whilst there is often a need to stay late to finish a particular task, try not to make this a regular occurrence.

Examine your expectations

What is holding you at your place of work? Do you find your work satisfying? Are you enjoying the tasks involved? What are the most stressful elements of the job and do the satisfactory elements of your work outweigh the awkward times? Is work affecting your quality of life or the quality of time you have for your personal life?

Change your eating habits

Diet can be a major factor in aiding relaxation and reducing stress, especially where food allergies or intolerances exist. Eating foods to which you are mildly intolerant can cause a range of unpleasant symptoms and add to the stress load for your body. As well as dealing with emotional stress, it will also have to cope with the physical stress of fighting off foods that are not beneficial to it.

REDUCE CAFFEINE INTAKE. Whilst caffeine is an effective stimulant when you are tired, its effects include raising your blood pressure and heart rate as well as other actions that mimic the alarm stage of the stress response. Caffeine's effects are long lasting. Try and restrict your caffeine intake to a couple of cups of tea, coffee or caffeinated soft drinks per day, or less if you are having difficulties sleeping.

INCREASE YOUR WATER INTAKE. Tiredness, fatigue and lethargy can be linked to dehydration. Increasing your water intake can help to improve these symptoms, and assist in improving your skin, reducing any oedema that has developed. Oedema in the tissues often develops during stressful times so that the body can maintain the higher blood pressure and has somewhere to store toxins produced as a result of a high intake of foods you are intolerant to.

⋀ Rehydrate
Drinking two litres of water a day can flush out toxins and reduce fatigue or lethargy.

REDUCE YOUR INTAKE OF FATTY FOODS. The temptation to snack on foods high in sugar or fat during times of stress is natural; your body wants the extra energy. However, such foods increase the stress on your body.

AVOID FOODS TO WHICH YOU ARE INTOLERANT. The most common allergens are wheat, dairy, nuts and eggs. Those with strong allergies to food substances will be aware of them, yet a mild intolerance can leave you with a range of uncomfortable physical and emotional symptoms. Identify any foods that disagree with you by keeping a diary of everything you eat and drink for two weeks and comparing it with your physical and emotional state.

EAT REGULARLY. Establishing regular mealtimes will bring additional control and structure to your life and ensure that your blood-sugar levels remain constant throughout the day.

CHEMICAL STRESSORS INCLUDE

Tea	Nicotine
Coffee	Sugar (especially refined sugars)
Cola-flavoured soft drinks	
Caffeine of any description	Foods high in fat
Alcohol	Sodium (salt)

Vitamin supplementation

A multi-vitamin can help to ensure that you are getting all the nutrients that you need to function effectively. Vitamins that are particularly useful for those experiencing high levels of stress include B vitamin complexes, and Vitamin C and zinc to support the immune system at this difficult time.

INCREASE YOUR INTAKE OF FRESH FOOD. Whilst you may look to pre-prepared meals to save time cooking, they do not provide you with the nutrients available in fresh foods. Cooking can

AVOID EATING WHERE YOU WORK. The temptation to continue working whilst eating will be huge. Give yourself the short breaks you deserve.

be a creative break from your routine. Look for recipes that require a short preparation time, and increase fruit and vegetable intake.

CUT BACK ON ALCOHOL. Although it appears to relax you, alcohol acts as a depressant to your nervous system, causes dehydration and, with extensive use, also raises blood pressure and heart rate. The current guidelines for alcohol consumption in the UK – that women should restrict their intake to 21 units per week and men to 28 units – is meant to be an upper limit. If you regularly drink that amount or more, reducing your intake is strongly advised.

≪ *Food for thought*
Homemade juices and a diet rich in fresh vegetables and fruits all help to provide essential vitamins and minerals to support a stressful lifestyle. Chocolate, unfortunately, doesn't.

10

Developing a stronger support network

The tend-and-befriend model (see page 7) for coping with stress and aiding relaxation does work and is an important area to look into. It is especially important if you feel cut off from others or that you lack support in your day-to-day life.

▼ *Play*
Life should not be a series of burdens. Learn from the children around you: make play a priority.

> *Help friends*
A shared activity, such as learning how to massage, can strengthen your network, provide a creative outlet and relieve stress all at the same time.

> *Social life*
Spend time with friends whose company you enjoy and with whom you can have fun.

Help with home life

If you or someone you know is having difficulties at home, social services may be able to help. Professional counsellors and a wide variety of complementary therapists also specialize in supporting you through stressful situations, aiding relaxation and suggesting ways of coping with stress.

IDENTIFY WHO YOU CAN TURN TO FOR HELP AND WHEN. You may have friends or family members who would be able and willing to help if you were in need. If you don't usually like to ask for help, it may be that they are unaware of your needs or that they don't actually know what they can do to help. Asking others for help is an effective way of including them in your life, making them feel wanted and useful.

LOOK AT PROFESSIONAL SUPPORT SERVICES. In the workplace this might include getting better access to administrative support, hiring a temporary assistant to get you through a difficult period or speaking to the human resources department if things are particularly difficult and you feel isolated from your colleagues.

CUT OUT THE DEAD WOOD. You may already be aware that some of the people you regularly associate with are not relaxing to be around. Whilst you may feel strong ties to them that you are not able or willing to give up, it may be necessary for you to limit contact with them for a while. This does not mean you should avoid seeing them ever again! Nor do you need a confrontation; simply become less available, fit contact with them into a specific task or activity that only goes on for a finite time. If you are aware that people turn to you for support above and beyond what you are currently able to provide, struggling to meet their needs can leave you feeling resentful and may not actually be serving them effectively either.

ENHANCE YOUR RELATIONSHIPS. Create good bonds with those who are able and willing to offer support. This must be a two-way relationship to be effective and of mutual benefit. Make sure that you are able to return that support in ways that they will appreciate and that make them feel cared for too. For instance, if childcare is a shared issue, offer to look after their children for the day so that they too can have time to relax.

< Ask for help
Identify friends or family members to whom you can really talk. Don't be afraid of asking others to help.

Index

Easy French Cooking

Styling DONNA HAY
Photography JON BADER

A J.B. Fairfax Press Publication

INTRODUCTION

In this book you will find recipes that retain the wonderful flavours of classic French cooking, but do not require the time, or contain the calories, of this popular cuisine. The emphasis is on fresh food that tastes wonderful, looks great and is easy to prepare.

The food is not 'nouvelle cuisine' but, rather, traditional French-style food adapted to suit today's lifestyles. The recipes are light, fresh and interesting, and use the healthier cooking techniques such as grilling, baking and poaching.

UK COOKERY EDITOR
Katie Swallow

EDITORIAL
Food Editor: Rachel Blackmore
Editorial and Production Assistant: Sheridan Packer
Editorial Coordinator: Margaret Kelly

Photography: Jon Bader
Styling: Donna Hay
Home Economist: Jody Vassallo

DESIGN AND PRODUCTION
Managers: Sheridan Carter, Anna Maguire
Layout and Design: Lulu Dougherty

COVER
Design: Chrissie Lloyd
Photography: Alan Newnham
Home Economist: Kathy Man
Styling: Kay McGlone

Published by J.B. Fairfax Press Pty Limited
80-82 McLachlan Avenue
Rushcutters Bay, NSW 2011, Australia
A.C.N. 003 738 430

Formatted by J.B. Fairfax Press Pty Limited
Printed by Toppan Printing Co, Hong Kong
PRINTED IN HONG KONG

JBFP 303 UK
Includes Index
ISBN 1 86343 142 X

Distributed by J.B. Fairfax Press Ltd
9 Trinity Centre, Park Farm Estate
Wellingborough, Northants
Ph: (0933) 402330 Fax: (0933) 402234

ABOUT THIS BOOK

INGREDIENTS

Unless otherwise stated the following ingredients are used in this book:

Cream — Double, suitable for whipping
Flour — White flour, plain or standard
Sugar — White sugar
Shallots — These are the French échalote.

If they are unavailable pickling onions can be used instead. See note on page 22 for more information on this vegetable.

In keeping with the true style of French cuisine wine has been used in some recipes in this book, in most cases stock can be used instead if you wish.

WHAT'S IN A TABLESPOON?

AUSTRALIA
1 tablespoon = 20 mL or 4 teaspoons
NEW ZEALAND
1 tablespoon = 15 mL or 3 teaspoons

UNITED KINGDOM

1 tablespoon = 15 mL or 3 teaspoons
The recipes in this book were tested in Australia where a 20 mL tablespoon is standard. The tablespoon in New Zealand and the United Kingdom sets of measuring spoons is 15 mL. For recipes using baking powder, gelatine, bicarbonate of soda, small quantities of flour and cornflour, simply add another teaspoon for each tablespoon specified.

CANNED FOODS

Can sizes vary between countries and manufacturers. You may find the quantities in this book are slightly different to what is available. Purchase and use the can size nearest to the suggested size in the recipe.

CONTENTS

SOUPS AND STARTERS

Soups and starters are the introduction to the meal, so they should be light and refreshing, but at the same time tempt the tastebuds. Many also make great light meals: serve soups with bread and other dishes with a green salad and bread.

VEGETABLE SOUP WITH PISTOU

1 tablespoon olive oil
2 onions, chopped
2 leeks, sliced
1 teaspoon chopped fresh thyme or
$^1/_2$ teaspoon dried thyme
3 stalks celery, sliced
2 large potatoes, diced
2 carrots, diced
2 zucchini (courgettes), sliced
250 g/8 oz green beans, cut into
2.5 cm/1 in pieces
440 g/14 oz canned lima, butter, red
kidney or mixed beans, drained
8 cups/2 litres/3$^1/_2$ pt water
freshly ground black pepper

PISTOU
1 bunch basil, leaves removed and
stems discarded
2 cloves garlic, chopped
125 g/4 oz Parmesan cheese, chopped
$^1/_4$ cup/60 mL/2 fl oz olive oil

1   Heat 1 tablespoon olive oil in a large saucepan over a medium heat, add onions, leeks and thyme and cook, stirring, for 5 minutes or until onions and leeks are soft.

2   Add celery, potatoes and carrots and cook, stirring, for 5 minutes. Add zucchini (courgettes), green beans, canned beans and water and bring to the boil. Reduce heat and simmer for 30 minutes or until vegetables are tender. Season to taste with black pepper.

3   To make Pistou, place basil, garlic, Parmesan cheese, $^1/_4$ cup/60 mL/2 fl oz olive oil and black pepper to taste in a food processor or blender and process to make a paste. Just prior to serving, stir Pistou into soup.

Serves 6

Vegetable Soup with Pistou, Garlic and Parsley Soup

Pistou is a condiment from the region of Provence. It is very similar to the Italian pesto and derives its name from the Italian word 'pestare' meaning to pound. The 'Pistou' can be stirred into the entire quantity of soup or each serving can be topped with a spoonful, alternatively, serve it separately and allow each person to help themselves.

GARLIC AND PARSLEY SOUP

A version of this soup is found in many of the countries that surround the Mediterranean. It is considered to be good for the liver, blood circulation and general health. Don't be put off by the amount of garlic used, you will find that because of the way the soup is cooked the garlic develops a subtle flavour and the end result is an exquisitely aromatic soup.

1 head garlic, cloves separated and unpeeled
6 cups/1.5 litres/2¹/₂ pt chicken or vegetable stock
¹/₄ teaspoon dried sage
¹/₄ teaspoon dried thyme
1 small bay leaf
3 sprigs fresh parsley
2 large potatoes, diced
pinch saffron powder
1 bunch fresh parsley, finely chopped
freshly ground black pepper

1 Bring a saucepan of water to the boil, add garlic cloves and boil for 30 seconds. Drain, rinse under cold running water and peel.

2 Place garlic, stock, sage, thyme, bay leaf and parsley sprigs in a large saucepan and bring to the boil. Reduce heat and simmer for 30 minutes.

3 Add potatoes and saffron to stock mixture and simmer for 15-20 minutes or until potatoes are tender. Remove bay leaf and discard. Remove pan from heat and set aside to cool slightly.

4 Place soup in batches in a food processor or blender and process until smooth. Return soup to a clean saucepan, bring to the boil and simmer for 2-3 minutes or until soup is hot. Stir in chopped parsley and season to taste with black pepper.

Serves 6

FRENCH ONION SOUP

Try serving this soup in the traditional French way, place one or two croûtes in a soup bowl or cup and pour the soup over.

15 g/¹/₂ oz butter
1 teaspoon olive oil
500 g/1 lb onions, thinly sliced
1 cup/250 mL/8 fl oz dry white wine
2 tablespoons flour
6 cups/1.5 litres/2¹/₂ pt hot beef stock
2 tablespoons brandy
freshly ground black pepper

CHEESE CROUTES
60 g/2 oz grated reduced-fat Cheddar cheese
30 g/1 oz grated Parmesan cheese
1 French breadstick, cut into thick slices

1 Heat butter and oil in a large saucepan over a medium heat. Add onions and cook, stirring, for 5 minutes. Stir in 2 tablespoons wine and cook over a low heat, stirring occasionally, and adding more wine as needed for 30-35 minutes or until onions are soft and golden.

2 Sprinkle flour over onion mixture and cook, stirring, for 1 minute longer. Gradually stir hot stock and remaining wine into pan and bring to the boil. Reduce heat and simmer for 15 minutes. Stir in brandy and season to taste with black pepper.

3 To make croûtes, place Cheddar cheese and Parmesan cheese in a small bowl and mix to combine. Place bread under a preheated medium grill and cook for 3-4 minutes or until toasted on one side. Sprinkle untoasted side of bread with cheese mixture and grill for 3-4 minutes or until cheese is melted and golden. Serve croûtes with soup.

Serves 6

WHITE BEAN SOUP

2 tablespoons olive oil
2 onions, sliced
2 leeks, sliced
2 bay leaves
$^1/_2$ teaspoon dried thyme
$^1/_2$ teaspoon dried sage
6 cups/1.5 litres/2$^1/_2$ pt chicken or
vegetable stock
315 g/10 oz canned lima or butter
beans, drained and rinsed
1 eggplant (aubergine), finely diced
440 g/14 oz canned tomatoes,
undrained and mashed
1 clove garlic, crushed
1 tablespoon chopped fresh parsley
1 tablespoon chopped fresh basil
1 tablespoon snipped fresh chives
freshly ground black pepper

1   Heat 2 teaspoons oil in a nonstick frying pan over a medium heat. Add onions, leeks, bay leaves, thyme, sage and 2 tablespoons stock and cook, stirring, for 5 minutes or until onions and leeks are soft.

2   Transfer onion mixture to a large saucepan, add remaining stock and beans and bring to the boil. Reduce heat and simmer for 15 minutes. Remove bay leaves and discard. Remove pan from heat and set aside to cool slightly.

3   Place bean mixture in batches in a food processor or blender and process until smooth. Return soup to a clean saucepan and set aside.

4   Heat remaining oil in a nonstick frying pan, add eggplant (aubergine) and cook over a medium heat, stirring, for 5 minutes or until eggplant (aubergine) is brown. Stir in tomatoes and garlic and bring to simmering. Cover and simmer for 10-15 minutes or until eggplant (aubergine) is tender.

5   Stir eggplant (aubergine) mixture, parsley, basil, chives and black pepper to taste into bean mixture, bring to simmering over a medium heat and cook, stirring frequently, for 10-15 minutes or until soup boils and is heated through.

Serves 6

This is a peasant-style soup and is a meal in itself. If you prefer a thinner soup add additional stock in step 5 to achieve the desired consistency.

French Onion Soup

Plate Villeroy & Boch

7

CHICKEN AND FRESH HERB TERRINE

Oven temperature
180°C, 350°F, Gas 4

1 bunch/500 g/1 lb spinach or
silverbeet
250 g/8 oz chicken livers, cleaned
1 tablespoon seasoned flour
15 g/1 oz butter
1 teaspoon olive oil
375 g/12 oz chicken meat, a mixture
of white and dark meat is best, minced
375 g/12 oz lean pork, minced
2 teaspoons finley chopped fresh
thyme or 1 teaspoon dried thyme
3 cloves garlic, crushed
2 onions, diced
1 tablespoon green peppercorns in
brine, drained
3 eggs
$^1/_2$ cup/125 mL/4 fl oz dry white wine
2 tablespoons port or sherry
3 tablespoons chopped fresh parsley
freshly ground black pepper

1   Boil, steam or microwave spinach
or silverbeet leaves to soften. Drain,
refresh under cold running water
and drain again. Line a lightly greased
terrine dish or a 11 x 21 cm/4$^1/_2$ x
8$^1/_2$ in loaf tin with overlapping
spinach leaves. Allow leaves to
overhang the sides.

2   Toss chicken livers in seasoned flour
to coat. Heat butter and oil in a frying
pan over a medium heat until foaming.
Add chicken livers and cook, stirring,
for 3-5 minutes or until they just
change colour. Remove livers from pan
and set aside to cool.

3   Chop chicken livers. Place chicken
livers, chicken, pork, thyme, garlic,
onions, green peppercorns, eggs, wine,
port or sherry, parsley and black pepper
to taste in a bowl and mix to combine.

4   Pack meat mixture into prepared
terrine dish or loaf tin, fold overhanging spinach leaves over filling and
cover with aluminium foil. Place
terrine dish or loaf tin in a baking dish
with enough boiling water to come
halfway up the sides of the dish and
bake for 2 hours. Drain off any juices,
cover top of terrine with foil, then
weight and set aside to cool. When
cold refrigerate overnight. To serve,
unmould and cut into slices.

Serves 10

The terrine will improve if
kept for 1-2 days before
serving. Accompanied by a
tossed salad of watercress
or rocket, a bowl of
gherkins and some French
bread this makes a truly
delicious starter or light
meal.

Chicken and Fresh Herb Terrine

SCALLOPS PROVENÇAL

2 teaspoons olive oil
1 onion, chopped
2 cloves garlic, crushed
440 g/14 oz canned tomatoes,
undrained and mashed
2 teaspoons finely chopped fresh
thyme or ¹/₂ teaspoon dried thyme
¹/₂ teaspoon dried oregano
500 g/1 lb scallops
2 tablespoons finely chopped
fresh parsley
freshly ground black pepper
30 g/1 oz reduced-fat Cheddar
cheese, grated

1   Heat oil in a nonstick frying pan over a medium heat, add onion and garlic and cook, stirring, for 3-4 minutes or until onion is soft. Stir in tomatoes, thyme and oregano and bring to the boil. Reduce heat and simmer for 10 minutes or until mixture reduces and thickens.

2   Add scallops, parsley and black pepper to taste and cook for 5 minutes. Divide scallop mixture between four scallop shells or shell-shaped dishes, sprinkle with Cheddar cheese and cook under a preheated hot grill for 4-5 minutes or until cheese melts and is golden.

Serves 4

The sauce for this dish should be very thick before adding the scallops as the juices from them will dilute it.

Plates Villeroy & Boch

Plate Country Road

Warm Asparagus Salad

500 g/1 lb asparagus, trimmed
1 teaspoon Dijon mustard
1 tablespoon red wine vinegar
3 tablespoons olive oil
freshly ground black pepper

1 Boil, steam or microwave asparagus until just tender. Drain well.

2 Place mustard, vinegar, oil and black pepper to taste in a small bowl and whisk to combine. Spoon dressing over warm asparagus and serve immediately.

Serves 4

This delightful warm salad makes a perfect start to a spring meal.

Left: Scallops Provençal
Above: Warm Asparagus Salad

WARM CHICKPEA SALAD

185 g/6 oz dried chickpeas
6 cups/1.5 litre/2¹/₂ pt vegetable or
chicken stock
1 clove garlic, crushed
1 sprig fresh thyme
2 bay leaves
1 onion, quartered
3 tablespoons chopped fresh parsley

FRESH THYME DRESSING
¹/₄ cup/60 mL/2 fl oz red wine vinegar
¹/₄ cup/60 mL/2 fl oz olive oil
2 teaspoons finely chopped fresh
thyme or ¹/₂ teaspoon dried thyme
1 clove garlic, crushed
1 small onion, thinly sliced
2 spring onions, finely chopped
freshly ground black pepper

Serves 6

1   Place chickpeas in a large bowl, cover with cold water and set aside to soak overnight. Drain. Place chickpeas, stock, garlic, thyme sprig, bay leaves and quartered onion in a large saucepan and bring to the boil. Boil for 10 minutes, then reduce heat and simmer for 45-60 minutes or until chickpeas are tender. Drain.

2   To make dressing, place vinegar, oil, thyme and garlic in a small bowl and whisk to combine. Add onion, spring onions and black pepper to taste and mix to combine.

3   Spoon dressing over warm chickpeas, toss to combine and sprinkle with parsley. Serve warm or at room temperature.

The secret to this recipe is to add the dressing to the warm chickpeas. If the chickpeas have been cooked in advance or you are using canned chickpeas, heat them before adding the dressing to achieve the best flavour.

TOMATO TART

1kg/2 lb small tomatoes, halved
8 sheets filo pastry
¹/₄ cup/60 mL/2 fl oz olive oil
1 tablespoon Dijon mustard
60 g/2 oz grated Parmesan cheese
2 tablespoons chopped fresh parsley
1 clove garlic, crushed
1 teaspoon chopped fresh thyme or
¹/₂ teaspoon dried thyme
1 teaspoon chopped fresh oregano or
¹/₂ teaspoon dried oregano
freshly ground black pepper
60 g/2 oz black olives, chopped

Makes 30

1   Place tomato halves on a wire rack set in a baking dish and bake for 30 minutes or until soft.

2   Layer filo pastry brushing between every second layer with oil. Place layered pastry in a nonstick 18 x 28 cm/7 x 11 in shallow cake tin, trim off excess and roll edges to form a rim.

3   Spread surface of pastry with mustard, sprinkle with Parmesan cheese and top with tomatoes. Place remaining oil, parsley, garlic, thyme, oregano and black pepper to taste in a bowl and toss to combine.

4   Sprinkle oil mixture over tomatoes, scatter with olives and bake for 15-20 minutes or until pastry is golden. Serve hot, warm or at room temperature, cut into bite-sized pieces.

Oven temperature
200°C, 400°F, Gas 6

This tart is delicious served with drinks prior to a meal or cut into larger pieces and accompanied by a salad as a starter.
The ideal tomatoes to use for this tart are plum (egg or Italian).

MIXED VEGETABLE PLATTER

Depending on the occasion the vegetables for this platter are prepared and arranged quite elegantly or for a more rustic approach they are left fairly chunky – it's really up to you. For casual outdoor entertaining use a flat wooden or colourful ceramic platter; for a more formal approach choose a large white ceramic serving platter.

250 g/8 oz small new potatoes
olive oil
freshly ground black pepper
125 g/4 oz green beans
250 g/8 oz asparagus spears, trimmed
60 g/2 oz snow peas (mangetout)
1 head broccoli, broken into
small florets
1 lettuce of your choice, leaves
separated
2 tomatoes, cut into wedges
1 red, green or yellow pepper, roasted
and cut into pieces
2 stalks celery, cut into matchsticks
Tapenade (recipe below)
1 French stick, sliced and toasted

RED WINE VINEGAR DRESSING
1/4 cup/60 mL/2 fl oz red wine vinegar
2 tablespoons olive oil
1 teaspoon Dijon mustard

1   Boil or microwave potatoes until just tender. Drain, place in a bowl and toss with 1 teaspoon oil and black pepper to taste. Set aside to cool.

2   Boil, steam or microwave beans, asparagus, snow peas (mangetout) and broccoli, separately, until just tender. Drain and refresh under cold running water.

3   Arrange potatoes, beans, asparagus, snow peas (mangetout), broccoli, lettuce, tomatoes, red, green or yellow pepper and celery, attractively, on a large serving platter. Cover and refrigerate for 1 hour or until ready to serve.

4   To make dressing, place vinegar, oil, mustard and black pepper to taste in a screwtop jar and shake well to combine. Drizzle dressing over vegetables and serve with Tapenade and toast.

Serves 8

TAPENADE

This olive pâté is so easy to make you will never bother buying it again. It is delicious served with raw or lightly cooked vegetables or spread on toast or crackers. It is also a nice alternative to butter as a spread on sandwiches.

125 g/4 oz pitted black olives
1 canned anchovy fillet, drained
1 tablespoon capers, drained and
rinsed
2 tablespoons olive oil
1 clove garlic, crushed
2 teaspoons lemon juice
3 tablespoons low-fat natural yogurt
freshly ground black pepper
1 tablespoon chopped fresh basil

1   Place olives, anchovy fillet, capers, oil, garlic and lemon juice in a food processor or blender and process to make a paste.

2   Transfer paste to a small bowl, add yogurt and black pepper to taste and mix to combine. Sprinkle with basil. Cover and chill for 1 hour or until ready to serve.

Makes 1/2 cup/125 mL/4 fl oz

Mixed Vegetable Platter, Tapenade

Plate Villeroy & Boch

FROM THE SEA

The coastline of France and especially that of the Mediterranean is rich in fish and seafood and it is from these areas that many of today's popular seafood dishes come. In this chapter you will find recipes ranging from rustic Bouillabaisse – a complete one-dish meal – to elegant Salmon Rolls with Tomato Butter – perfect for a formal dinner party.

BOUILLABAISSE

3 kg/6 lb mixed fish and seafood,
including firm white fish fillets, prawns,
mussels, crab and calamari (squid) rings
$^{1}/_{4}$ cup/60 mL/2 fl oz olive oil
2 cloves garlic, crushed
2 large onions, chopped
2 leeks, sliced
2 x 440 g/14 oz canned tomatoes,
undrained and mashed
1 tablespoon chopped fresh thyme or 1
teaspoon dried thyme
2 tablespoons chopped fresh basil or $1^{1}/_{2}$
teaspoons dried basil
2 tablespoons chopped fresh parsley
2 bay leaves
2 tablespoons finely grated orange rind
1 teaspoon saffron threads
1 cup/250 mL/8 fl oz dry white wine
1 cup/250 mL/8 fl oz fish stock
freshly ground black pepper

1   Remove bones and skin from fish fillets and cut into 2 cm/$^{3}/_{4}$ in cubes. Peel and devein prawns, leaving tails intact. Scrub and remove beards from mussels. Cut crab into quarters. Set side.

2   Heat oil in a large saucepan over a medium heat, add garlic, onions and leeks and cook for 5 minutes or until onions are golden. Add tomatoes, thyme, basil, parsley, bay leaves, orange rind, saffron, wine and stock and bring to the boil. Reduce heat and simmer for 30 minutes.

3   Add fish and crab and cook for 10 minutes, add remaining seafood and cook for 5 minutes longer or until fish and seafood are cooked. Season to taste with black pepper.

Serves 6

Originally cooked on the beach by fishermen, Bouillabaisse is one of the best known and most popular fish soups. It can be made using whatever seafood is available so use this recipe as a guide only. For a complete meal accompany with crusty French bread and a glass of dry white wine.

Saucepan and bowls Accoutrement

Bouillabaisse

16

Above: Fish en Papillote
Right: Salad Niçoise

FISH EN PAPILLOTE

Oven temperature
200°C, 400°F, Gas 6

4 red snapper or bream fillets
1 egg white, lightly beaten
1 carrot, cut into thin strips
1 leek, cut into thin strips
1 red pepper, cut into thin strips
4 sprigs fresh lemon thyme or thyme
freshly ground black pepper

HERB MARINADE
2 tablespoons olive oil
1 tablespoon white wine vinegar
1 tablespoon finely chopped fresh dill
1 tablespoon snipped fresh chives

Part of the fun of this dish is serving it to the table still wrapped and allowing each person to enjoy the wonderful aromas that are released when the parcel is opened.

1 To make marinade, place oil, vinegar, dill and chives in a small bowl and mix to combine. Place fish in a shallow glass or ceramic dish, pour over marinade, cover and set aside to marinate for 2 hours. Drain well.

2 Cut four circles of nonstick baking paper large enough to completely enclose the fillets. The paper should be at least 10 cm/4 in larger than the fillets on all sides. Fold paper in half lengthwise and cut a half-heart shape. Open out paper and brush edges with egg white.

3 Place a fillet on one half of each paper heart, near the centre fold line, then top with carrot, leek, red pepper, a sprig of thyme and black pepper to taste. Fold other half of paper over ingredients and roll edges to seal. Place paper parcels on a baking tray and bake for 20 minutes or until fish flakes when tested with a fork.

Serves 4

18

Salad Niçoise

1 lettuce of your choice, leaves separated
500 g/1 lb fresh young broad
beans, shelled
1 large red pepper, cut into thin strips
8 marinated artichoke hearts, halved
250 g/8 oz cherry tomatoes
1 large cucumber, cut into strips
3 spring onions, chopped
12 canned anchovy fillets, drained
250 g/8 oz canned tuna
in water, drained
185 g/6 oz marinated black olives
6 hard-boiled eggs, quartered
1/4 cup/60 mL/2 fl oz olive oil
freshly ground black pepper

Arrange lettuce leaves, beans, red pepper, artichokes, tomatoes, cucumber, spring onions, anchovy fillets, tuna, olives and eggs on a large serving platter or in a large salad bowl. Drizzle with oil and season to taste with black pepper.

Serves 4-6

This is an easy spring or summer dish. As the broad beans are eaten raw it must be made with very fresh young beans. It should be noted that there are many versions of this salad and that the traditional salad does not include potatoes or other cooked vegetables.

SEAFOOD WITH GREEN VEGETABLES

100 g/3^1/$_2$ oz snow peas (mangetout)
250 g/8 oz broccoli, broken into small florets
250 g/8 oz asparagus spears, trimmed
1^1/$_2$ cups/375 mL/12 fl oz fish stock
250 g/8 oz large uncooked prawns, shelled and deveined, tails intact
250 g/8 oz firm white fish fillets, cut into 2 cm/^{3}/$_4$ in cubes
250 g/8 oz scallops
^{1}/$_2$ cup/125 mL/4 fl oz cream (double)
^{1}/$_4$ cup/60 mL/2 fl oz tomato purée
1 tablespoon chopped fresh tarragon or 1 teaspoon dried tarragon
freshly ground black pepper

1   Steam or microwave snow peas (mangetout), broccoli and asparagus, separately, until just tender. Drain, refresh under cold running water and set aside.

2   Place stock in a large saucepan and bring to the boil, add prawns, fish and scallops to stock and cook for 5 minutes or until just cooked. Using a slotted spoon remove and set aside.

3   Stir in cream, tomato purée and tarragon and bring to the boil. Reduce heat and simmer for 10 minutes or until liquid is reduced by one-third. Add reserved vegetables and seafood to sauce and cook for 1-2 minutes or until heated through. Season to taste with black pepper and serve immediately.

Serves 4

All that this delightful fish and vegetable dish needs to make a complete meal is Wild Rice Pilau (page 59).

MUSSELS IN WINE AND GARLIC

30 g/1 oz butter
4 pickling onions or shallots, finely chopped
3 cloves garlic, crushed
2 cups/500 mL/16 fl oz white wine
1 cup/250 mL/8 fl oz fish stock
2 kg/4 lb mussels, scrubbed and beards removed
freshly ground black pepper
2 tablespoons finely chopped fresh parsley

1   Melt butter in a large saucepan over a medium heat, add onions or shallots and garlic and cook, stirring, for 5 minutes or until onions or shallots are golden. Add wine and stock, bring to the boil, then reduce heat and simmer for 10 minutes.

2   Add mussels and cook for 5 minutes or until shells open. Discard any mussels that do not open after 5 minutes cooking. Using a slotted spoon remove mussels from liquid and place in a serving dish. Season sauce to taste with black pepper, pour over mussels and sprinkle with parsley.

Serves 4

Mussels in Wine and Garlic, Seafood with Green Vegetables and Wild Rice Pilau

Mussels will live out of water for up to 7 days if treated correctly. To keep mussels alive, place them in a bucket, cover with a wet towel and top with ice. Store in a cool place and as the ice melts, drain off the water and replace the ice. It is important that the mussels do not sit in the water or they will drown.

LEEK AND SPINACH FISH PARCELS

8 spinach or silverbeet leaves
3 leeks, cut in half lengthwise
4 boneless white fish fillets, skinned
and chopped
2 spring onions, chopped
1 clove garlic, crushed
$^1/_4$ teaspoon saffron threads, soaked in 1
tablespoon of hot water

WHITE WINE AND
GINGER SAUCE
15 g/$^1/_2$ oz butter
2 pickling onions or shallots, chopped
1 tablespoon finely grated fresh ginger
1 cup/250 mL/8 fl oz fish stock
$^1/_4$ cup/60 mL/2 fl oz dry white wine
$^1/_4$ cup/60 mL/2 fl oz cream (double)

1 Blanch spinach or silverbeet leaves in boiling water for 1-2 minutes or until just tender. Drain, rinse under cold running water and pat dry with absorbent kitchen paper. Set aside.

2 Blanch leeks in boiling water for 1-2 minutes or until just tender. Drain and rinse under cold running water. Separate leaves and pat dry with absorbent kitchen paper. Set aside.

3 Place fish, spring onions, garlic and saffron mixture in a food processor and process until smooth.

4 Place 2 tablespoons fish mixture in the centre of each spinach leaf, fold in sides and wrap to form individual parcels. Repeat with leeks leaves and remaining fish mixture.

5 Place parcels in a steamer, set over a saucepan of simmering water and steam for 10 minutes or until fish is cooked.

6 To make sauce, melt butter in a frying pan over a medium heat, add onions or shallots and ginger and cook, stirring, for 3 minutes. Stir in stock, wine and cream and bring to the boil. Reduce heat and simmer for 10 minutes or until sauce is reduced by one-third. Serve with fish parcels.

Serves 4

Shallots when used in this book refer to the French échalote. These are related to the onion but have a more delicate flavour. They are extremely popular in French cooking and have been grown in France since about 800 AD.

Plate Accoutrement

Left: Leek and Spinach Fish Parcels
Right: Salmon Rolls with Tomato Butter

Cutlery Orrefors Kosta Boda

SALMON ROLLS WITH TOMATO BUTTER

125 g/4 oz low-fat ricotta or curd
cheese, drained
1 tablespoon chopped fresh dill
2 teaspoons lime juice
1 tablespoon finely grated lime rind
freshly ground black pepper
500 g/1 lb salmon fillet, boned and
skinned
$^1/_2$ bunch/125 g/4 oz watercress, broken
into sprigs

TOMATO BUTTER
4 ripe tomatoes
sea salt
30 g/1 oz butter

1   To make Tomato Butter, cut tomatoes
in half lengthwise and place on a lightly
greased baking tray. Sprinkle with salt
and bake for 30 minutes or until tomatoes
are very soft. Remove tomatoes from oven
and set aside to cool slightly. Place warm

tomatoes and butter in a food processor or
blender and process until smooth.

2   Place ricotta or curd cheese, dill, lime
juice, lime rind and black pepper to taste
in a food processor or blender and process
until smooth.

3   Cut salmon into four 3 cm/1$^1/_4$ in wide
strips. Spread each strip with some of the
ricotta mixture, roll up and secure with
wooden toothpicks or cocktail sticks.
Place rolls on a lightly greased baking tray,
cover and bake for 15 minutes or until fish
is cooked.

4   To serve, divide watercress between
four serving plates, top with a salmon roll.
Serve immediately drizzled with Tomato
Butter.

Serves 4

Oven temperature
180°C, 350°F, Gas 4

An elegant yet easy dinner
party dish that is sure to
impress. The rolls can be
prepared several hours in
advance, placed on the
baking tray, covered and
refrigerated until ready to
cook.

CHICKEN PLUS

In this chapter there is an imaginative selection of poultry and game recipes. Traditional recipes such as Coq au Vin and Chicken Chasseur are made using considerably less fat, yet retain their authentic flavours.

CHICKEN WITH MUSHROOMS

Oven temperature
180°C, 350°F, Gas 4

4 boneless chicken breast fillets
freshly ground black pepper
1 tablespoon walnut or olive oil
8 cloves garlic, peeled
250 g/8 oz mixed mushrooms
1 tablespoon chopped fresh sage or 1
teaspoon dried sage
$^1/_4$ cup/60 mL/2 fl oz dry white wine
1 cup/250 mL/8 fl oz chicken stock
$^1/_2$ cup/125 mL/4 fl oz cream (double)

1   Season chicken with black pepper and brush with oil. Place chicken and garlic in a flameproof baking dish and bake for 40 minutes or until chicken is tender. Remove chicken from dish, set aside and keep warm.

2   Skim fat from juices in dish, add mushrooms and sage. Place dish over a medium heat and cook, stirring, for 5 minutes or until mushrooms are tender. Remove mushrooms from pan, set aside and keep warm. Add wine, stock and cream to pan and bring to the boil. Reduce heat and simmer for 10 minutes or until sauce is reduced by one-third. Season to taste with black pepper. To serve, spoon sauce over chicken and accompany with mushrooms.

Serves 4

If you can only get ordinary mushrooms, add a few dried mushrooms for extra flavour. You will need to soak the dried mushrooms in warm water for 20 minutes or until they are soft. Drain well, then slice or chop and add to the fresh mushrooms when cooking. Dried mushrooms have a strong flavour and you only need a few to add flavour.

*Chicken with Mushrooms,
Chicken Cassoulet*

Plates Villeroy & Boch

CHICKEN CASSOULET

Oven temperature
200°C, 400°F, Gas 6

750 g/1¹/₂ lb dried haricot or
borlotti beans
2 tablespoons olive oil
1 kg/2 lb chicken thigh or breast fillets,
cut into 2 cm/³/₄ in cubes
2 cloves garlic, thinly sliced
2 onions, chopped
2 leeks, sliced
250 g/8 oz salami, chopped
2 x 440 g/14 oz canned tomatoes,
undrained and mashed
¹/₂ cup/125 mL/4 fl oz dry white wine
1 bouquet garni
freshly ground black pepper
2 cups/125 g/4 oz wholemeal
breadcrumbs, made from stale bread

Beans are an essential
ingredient for any cassoulet
as they give the dish its
characteristic creaminess
and flavour. For a quicker
version of this dish canned
beans can be used.

1   Place beans in a large bowl, cover with
water and set aside to soak overnight,
then drain. Place beans in a large saucepan with enough water to cover and bring
to the boil. Boil for 10 minutes, then
reduce heat and simmer for 1 hour or until
beans are tender. Drain and set aside.

2   Heat oil in a large saucepan over a
medium heat, add chicken and cook,
stirring, for 10 minutes or until chicken is
brown on all sides. Remove from pan and
drain on absorbent kitchen paper.

3   Add garlic, onions and leeks to pan
and cook, stirring, for 5 minutes or until
onions are golden. Add salami, tomatoes,
wine and bouquet garni and bring to the
boil. Reduce heat and simmer for 10
minutes. Return chicken to pan, cover
and simmer for 30 minutes or until
chicken is tender. Season to taste with
black pepper.

4   Spoon half the chicken mixture into a
large casserole dish and top with half the
beans. Repeat with remaining chicken
mixture and beans to use all ingredients.
Sprinkle with breadcrumbs and bake,
uncovered, for 30 minutes or until hot
and bubbling and top is golden.

Serves 6

BLACKCURRANT PHEASANT

Oven temperature
180°C, 350°F, Gas 4

1.5 kg/3 lb pheasant, quartered
freshly ground black pepper
¹/₂ cup/125 mL/4 fl oz water
1 tablespoon olive oil
2 tablespoons blackcurrant conserve
¹/₂ cup/125 mL/4 fl oz orange juice
1 cup/250 mL/8 fl oz chicken stock
¹/₂ cup/125 mL/4 fl oz red wine

This is a simple yet tasty
method of preparing
pheasant. It is delicious
served with Glazed
Vegetables (page 58).

1   Season pheasant with black pepper
and place on a rack set in a heatproof
baking dish. Pour water into dish.

2   Place oil, conserve and orange juice in
a small bowl and mix to combine. Brush
pheasant with conserve mixture and bake,

basting frequently, for 40 minutes or until
pheasant is tender. Remove pheasant
from pan, cover, set aside and keep warm.

3   Skim fat from pan juices, add stock
and wine and any remaining conserve
mixture to pan, place over a medium heat
and bring to the boil, stirring constantly,
for 3-4 minutes or until sauce reduces and
thickens slightly. Pour sauce over
pheasant and serve immediately.

Serves 4

Blackcurrant Pheasant, Glazed Vegetables

Plates Villeroy & Boch Glasses Orrefors Kosta Boda

Plate Accoutrement

Above: Rabbit with Thyme and Mustard
Right: Coq au Vin

Rabbit and mustard are traditional companions – this recipe is a variation of a popular 17th-century French dish – rabbit stew in mustard sauce.

RABBIT WITH THYME AND MUSTARD

2 tablespoons olive oil
1 kg/2 lb rabbit, cut into pieces
3 tablespoons Dijon mustard
3 cups/750 mL/1¼ pt chicken stock
½ cup/125 mL/4 fl oz red wine
6 sprigs fresh thyme or 1 teaspoon dried thyme
250 g/8 oz small new potatoes
freshly ground black pepper

1 Heat oil in a large saucepan over a medium heat, add rabbit and cook, turning frequently, for 10 minutes or until brown on all sides.

2 Add mustard, stock, wine and thyme to pan and bring to the boil. Reduce heat, cover and simmer, stirring occasionally, for 1½ hours or until rabbit is tender. Add potatoes and cook for 30 minutes longer or until potatoes are tender. Season to taste with black pepper.

Serves 4

Coq au Vin

2 kg/4 lb chicken pieces
$^{1}/_{2}$ cup/60 g/2 oz seasoned flour
2 tablespoons olive oil
2 cloves garlic, crushed
12 pickling onions or shallots, peeled
8 rashers bacon, chopped
1 cup/250 mL/8 fl oz chicken stock
3 cups/750 mL/1$^{1}/_{4}$ pt red wine
250 g/8 oz button mushrooms
freshly ground black pepper

Serves 6

1   Toss chicken in flour to coat. Shake off excess flour and set aside.

2   Heat oil in a large nonstick frying pan over a medium heat and cook chicken in batches, turning frequently, for 10 minutes or until brown on all sides. Remove chicken from pan and drain on absorbent kitchen paper.

3   Add garlic, onions or shallots and bacon to pan and cook, stirring, for 5 minutes or until onions are golden. Return chicken to pan, stir in stock and wine and bring to the boil. Reduce heat, cover and simmer, stirring occasionally, for 1$^{1}/_{4}$ hours or until chicken is tender. Add mushrooms and black pepper to taste and cook for 10 minutes longer.

Serve Coq au Vin with Braised Artichokes and Beans (page 56) and steamed new potatoes.

DUCK WITH RATATOUILLE

1 tablespoon olive oil
1.5 kg/3 lb duck, cut into pieces
2 cloves garlic, crushed
1 large onion, cut into wedges
1 large red pepper, chopped
1 large green pepper, chopped
125 g/4 oz button mushrooms, halved
440 g/14 oz canned tomatoes, undrained
and mashed
100 g/3^1/$_2$ oz dried figs
3 sprigs fresh thyme or ^{1}/$_2$ teaspoon
dried thyme
2 tablespoons chopped fresh basil or
1 teaspoon dried basil
2 cups/500 mL/16 fl oz chicken stock
^{1}/$_4$ cup/60 mL/2 fl oz red wine

1   Heat oil in a large saucepan over a medium heat, add duck and cook, turning frequently, for 10 minutes or until brown on all sides. Remove duck from pan and drain on absorbent kitchen paper.

2   Add garlic and onion to pan and cook, stirring, for 3 minutes or until onion is golden. Add red pepper, green pepper and mushrooms and cook for 5 minutes longer. Stir tomatoes, figs, thyme, basil, stock and wine into pan and bring to the boil. Reduce heat and simmer for 10 minutes.

3   Return duck to pan, cover and cook over a medium heat for 40 minutes or until duck is tender.

Serves 4

For a complete meal serve this tasty duck dish with Wild Rice Pilau (page 59) or Potato and Cheese Pancake (page 60).

DUCK A L'ORANGE

Oven temperature
180°C, 350°F, Gas 4

2 kg/4 lb duck
freshly ground black pepper
2 sprigs fresh rosemary or ^{1}/$_2$ teaspoon
dried rosemary
2 sprigs fresh thyme or ^{1}/$_2$ teaspoon
dried thyme
1 clove garlic, crushed
1 tablespoon olive oil
2 cups/500 mL/16 fl oz orange juice
1 tablespoon finely grated orange rind
1 tablespoon brown sugar
3 oranges, segmented and all white pith
removed
2 tablespoons brandy

1   Season duck with black pepper and place rosemary, thyme and garlic in cavity. Pierce skin of duck several times with a fork and brush with oil. Place duck on a wire rack set in a heatproof baking dish and bake for 1 hour or until tender. Remove duck from pan, cover, set aside and keep warm.

2   Skim fat from pan juices, stir in orange juice, orange rind, sugar, orange segments and brandy and bring to the boil. Reduce heat and simmer, stirring, for 10 minutes or until sauce is reduced by one-third.

3   To serve, carve duck, arrange on a serving platter and pour over sauce.

Serves 6

Duck with Ratatouille, Duck à L'Orange

This recipe is a modern version of an old favourite – the richness of the duck is balanced by the tartness of the orange. Serve it with a steamed green vegetable and small new potatoes.

CHICKEN IN APPLE CIDER

1 tablespoon olive oil
2 cloves garlic, crushed
10 pickling onions or shallots
4 boneless chicken breast fillets
3 tablespoons fresh tarragon leaves or 1 tablespoon dried tarragon
1 cup/250 mL/8 fl oz apple cider
1 cup/250 mL/8 fl oz chicken stock
$^1/_4$ cup/60 mL/2 fl oz dry white wine
1 tablespoon tarragon or white wine vinegar
1 cup/200 g/6$^1/_2$ oz low-fat natural yogurt
freshly ground black pepper

If you do not have apple cider, sparkling or still apple juice can be used instead.

1 Heat oil in a large frying pan over a medium heat, add garlic and onions or shallots and cook, stirring, for 5 minutes. Add chicken and cook, turning, for 10 minutes or until golden on all sides.

2 Add tarragon, cider, stock, wine and vinegar to pan and bring to the boil. Reduce heat, cover and simmer for 30 minutes or until chicken is tender. Remove pan from heat, stir in yogurt and season to taste with black pepper.

Serves 4

Plate Limoges Australia

Plate Villeroy & Boch *Cutlery Orrefors Kosta Boda*

CHICKEN CHASSEUR

1 tablespoon olive oil
1.5 kg/3 lb chicken pieces
¹/₂ cup/125 mL/4 fl oz dry white wine
2 cups/500 mL/16 fl oz chicken stock
3 tablespoons tomato paste (purée)
2 tablespoons brandy
1 tablespoon chopped fresh parsley
1 tablespoon chopped fresh tarragon
125 g/4 oz mushrooms, sliced
freshly ground black pepper

1   Heat oil in a large saucepan over a medium heat and cook chicken in batches, turning frequently, for 10 minutes or until brown on all sides. Remove chicken from pan and drain on absorbent kitchen paper.

2   Stir wine, stock, tomato paste (purée), brandy, parsley and tarragon into pan and bring to the boil. Return chicken to pan, reduce heat, cover and simmer, stirring occasionally, for 1 hour.

3   Add mushrooms to pan and cook for 20 minutes longer or until chicken is tender. Season to taste with black pepper.

Chasseur denotes a sautéed dish with a sauce made from mushrooms, tomatoes and white wine.

Left: Chicken in Apple Cider
Above: Chicken Chasseur

Serves 6

MEAT DISHES

The selection of meat recipes in this chapter shows the diversity of French cooking. Pot-au-Feu is wonderful for feeding a crowd, while Sausages with Onions and Wine is a perfect family meal and Pork with Vinegar and Herbs an easy dish for mid-week entertaining.

FRUIT-FILLED PORK

Oven temperature
220°C, 425°F, Gas 7

1 rack of pork, containing 8 cutlets
500 g/1 lb blueberries or blackcurrants
freshly ground black pepper
1 tablespoon olive oil
1 cup/250 mL/8 fl oz dry white wine

1 Using a sharp knife, separate bones from meat, leaving both ends intact, to make a pocket. Trim excess fat from outside of rack.

2 Place blueberries or blackcurrants in a bowl and season to taste with black pepper. Place half the fruit mixture in pocket of meat and place in a flameproof baking dish. Brush pork with oil and bake for 20 minutes. Reduce oven temperature to 200°C/400°F/Gas 6 and bake for 1 hour longer or until cooked. Remove meat from pan, place on a warm serving platter, cover with foil and set aside to stand for 15-20 minutes.

3 Add wine and remaining fruit to baking dish and bring to the boil over a medium heat. Reduce heat and simmer, stirring constantly and scraping base of dish, for 10 minutes or until sauce is reduced by half. Serve sauce with pork.

Serves 8

A tasty and easy dish that can use a variety of fruit. Try cherries, redcurrants or plums instead of the blueberries or blackcurrants.

Fruit-filled Pork, Steak Bordelaise

STEAK BORDELAISE

6 fillet or rib-eye steaks
6 spring onions, chopped
1 clove garlic, crushed
1 cup/250 mL/8 fl oz beef stock
¹/₂ cup/125 mL/4 fl oz dry red wine
freshly ground black pepper

This dish takes little time or effort to prepare and is excellent for mid-week entertaining. It is delicious served with Potato Gratin (page 57) and Glazed Vegetables (page 58).

1   Heat a nonstick frying pan over a medium heat, add steaks and cook for 3-4 minutes each side or until cooked to your liking. Remove steaks from pan, set aside and keep warm.

2   Add spring onions, garlic and 2 tablespoons stock to pan and cook, stirring, for 2-3 minutes. Remove spring onions from pan and set aside. Add remaining stock and wine to pan, bring to the boil and boil for 5-10 minutes or until sauce reduces and thickens. Return spring onions to pan and season to taste with black pepper. Serve sauce with steak.

Serves 6

PORK FILLET EN PAPILLOTE

Oven temperature
220°C, 425°F, Gas 7

1 tablespoon olive oil
1 teaspoon dried sage
freshly ground black pepper
2 x 375 g/12 oz pork fillets, trimmed of all visible fat
2 leeks, cut into thin strips
1 carrot, cut into thin strips
2 stalks celery, cut into thin strips
¹/₂ cup/125 mL/4 fl oz dry white wine

APRICOT SAUCE
250 g/8 oz dried apricots, chopped
2 cups/500 mL/16 fl oz sweet white wine

This dish can be prepared up to the end of step 4 several hours ahead of time. The sauce can also be made in advance.

1   Place oil, sage and black pepper to taste in a small bowl or cup and mix to combine. Rub oil mixture over pork fillets and set aside for 30 minutes.

2   Heat a nonstick frying pan over a medium heat, add pork fillets and cook, turning, for 5 minutes or until brown on all sides. Remove fillets from pan and set aside to cool.

3   Add leeks, carrot and celery to pan and cook, stirring, for 2-3 minutes. Stir in 2 tablespoons wine and continue cooking,

adding wine and stirring occasionally, for 10 minutes or until vegetables are soft.

4   Cut two pieces nonstick baking paper large enough to completely enclose fillets. The paper should be a least 10 cm/4 in larger than fillets on all sides. Fold paper in half lengthwise and cut a half-heart shape. Open out paper. Place half the vegetable mixture and one fillet on one half of each paper heart, near the centre fold line. Sprinkle with remaining wine and season to taste with black pepper. Fold other half of paper over ingredients and roll edges to seal.

5   Place paper parcels on a baking tray and bake for 20 minutes or until cooked.

6   To make sauce, place apricots and wine in a small saucepan and bring to the boil over a medium heat. Remove pan from heat and set aside to soak for 20 minutes. Place apricot and wine mixture in a food processor or blender and process until smooth. Serve with pork.

Serves 6

PORK WITH VINEGAR AND HERBS

*Pork with Vinegar and Herbs,
Pork Fillet en Papillote*

1 tablespoon chopped fresh thyme or
1 teaspoon dried thyme
1 tablespoon chopped fresh sage or
1 teaspoon dried sage
1 tablespoon vegetable oil
4 pork loin chops, trimmed of
all visible fat
$^1/_2$ cup/125 mL/4 fl oz red wine vinegar
freshly ground black pepper
2 tablespoons chopped fresh parsley or
basil

1   Place thyme, sage and oil in a shallow glass or ceramic dish and mix to combine. Add chops to herb mixture and turn to coat. Cover and set aside to marinate for 1 hour.

2   Heat a nonstick frying pan over a medium heat, add chops and cook for 3-4 minutes each side or until brown. Stir in vinegar, reduce heat and simmer for 25-30 minutes or until pork is tender and vinegar reduced. Season to taste with black pepper and sprinkle with parsley or basil.

Serves 4

Add a little water during cooking if the dish becomes too dry.

37

Above: Making Pot-au-Feu
Right: Navarin Lamb

POT-AU-FEU

2-2.5 kg/4-5 lb topside of beef
1 onion, studded with 4 cloves
1/2 teaspoon black peppercorns
2 cloves garlic
1 bouquet garni
4 large potatoes, quartered
4 large carrots, cut into 5 cm/2 in pieces
4 parsnips, cut into 5 cm/2 in pieces
8 stalks celery, cut into 5 cm/2 in pieces
4 thin leeks, cut into 5 cm/2 in pieces
1/2 cup/125 mL/4 fl oz red wine

This is a wonderfully economical dish to make for a crowd. Serve the meat, vegetables and broth together in soup plates. Accompany with French bread and a selection of mustards and pickles.
If you can prepare this dish to the end of step 1 the day before, then about 1 hour before serving, remove the layer of fat that has set on the surface, bring to the boil and complete as described in recipe.

Serves 8

1   Place beef, clove-studded onion, black peppercorns, garlic and bouquet garni in a large saucepan. Add cold water to cover and bring to the boil over a medium heat, remove any scum as necessary. Reduce heat, cover and simmer for 2½-3 hours.

2   Add potatoes, carrots, parsnips, celery and leeks to pan and simmer for 20-30 minutes or until vegetables are tender.

3   Remove meat and vegetables from cooking liquid, set aside and keep warm.

4   Strain cooking liquid and discard clove-studded onion, black peppercorns, garlic and bouquet garni. Return cooking liquid to saucepan, add wine, bring to the boil and simmer for 5 minutes. To serve, slice meat and arrange with vegetables on a large serving platter. Place cooking liquid in a soup tureen and pass separately.

Navarin Lamb

6 lamb noisettes or loin chops
1 onion, sliced
1 clove garlic, crushed
1 teaspoon chopped fresh rosemary or
$^1/_2$ teaspoon dried rosemary
440 g/14 oz canned tomatoes, undrained
and mashed
1 cup/250 mL/8 fl oz chicken stock
$^1/_2$ cup/125 mL/4 fl oz dry red wine
12 small new potatoes
12 pickling onions or shallots
6 small carrots, scrubbed
250 g/8 oz green beans, cut into 5 cm/
2 in pieces
freshly ground black pepper

1 Heat a nonstick frying pan over a medium heat, add lamb and cook for 3-4 minutes each side or until brown. Remove lamb from pan and place in a casserole dish.

2 Add sliced onion, garlic, rosemary and 1 tablespoon juice from tomatoes to pan and cook over a medium heat, stirring, for 5 minutes or until onion is soft. Stir tomatoes, stock and wine into pan, bring to the boil, then reduce heat and simmer for 15 minutes or until mixture reduces and thickens. Add sauce to casserole, cover and bake for 1 hour. Add potatoes and pickling onions or shallots to casserole and bake for 1 hour longer or until meat and vegetables are tender.

3 Boil or microwave carrots and beans until just tender, drain and refresh under cold running water. Add carrots and beans to casserole and bake for 20 minutes longer. Season to taste with black pepper.

Serves 6

Oven temperature
180°C, 350°F, Gas 4

Lamb noisettes are rolled, boneless loin chops. The meat is rolled up tightly and tied. These are readily available in the meat section of your supermarket and you will find that most butchers are happy to prepare noisettes for you if you order them in advance.

BEEF BOURGUIGNON

1 kg/2 lb chuck steak, trimmed of all
visible fat and cut into 2.5 cm/1 in cubes
2 cups/500 mL/16 fl oz dry red wine
1 teaspoon chopped fresh thyme
2 cloves garlic, crushed
1 bay leaf
1 tablespoon olive oil
2 rashers bacon, trimmed of all visible
fat and chopped
250 g/8 oz button mushrooms
12 pickling onions or shallots
1 cup/250 mL/8 fl oz beef stock
$^1/_2$ cup/125 mL/4 fl oz tomato purée
2 tablespoons brandy
2 teaspoons cornflour blended with 2
tablespoons water
freshly ground black pepper

*This classic French stew is
even better if you have time
to marinate it in the red wine
and herbs overnight.*

1   Combine beef, wine, thyme, garlic and
bay leaf in a glass or ceramic bowl, cover
and marinate for 30 minutes. Remove
beef from wine mixture and pat dry.
Reserve wine mixture.

2   Heat oil in a large saucepan over a
high heat, add beef and bacon and cook
in batches for 5 minutes or until brown.
Remove beef mixture from pan, drain on
absorbent kitchen paper and set aside.

3   Add mushrooms and onions or
shallots to pan and cook, stirring, for 5
minutes or until onions or shallots are
brown. Remove mushrooms and onions
from pan and set aside.

4   Return beef mixture to pan, stir in
stock, tomato purée and reserved wine
mixture, bring to simmering, cover and
simmer for $1^1/_2$ hours or until beef is
tender. Return mushrooms and onions or
shallots to pan, stir in brandy and
cornflour mixture, cover and simmer for
30 minutes longer. Season to taste with
black pepper.

Serves 6

SAUSAGES WITH ONIONS AND WINE

8 thin sausages of your choice
2 large onions, thinly sliced
1 clove garlic, crushed
1 cup/250 mL/8 fl oz dry white wine
freshly ground black pepper

*You can make this dish using
any type of sausage. If
chicken or turkey sausages
are available use these as
they are lower in fat than
traditional meat based
sausages. For a complete
meal serve with Fennel Pea
Purée (page 56) and
mashed potatoes or crusty
bread.*

1   Heat a nonstick frying pan over a
medium heat, add sausages and cook,
turning until brown on all sides and
almost cooked. Remove from pan and
drain on absorbent kitchen paper.

2   Add onions, garlic and 2 tablespoons
wine to pan and cook, stirring and adding
wine as necessary for 15-20 minutes or
until onions are very soft and golden.

3   Return sausages to pan, stir in
remaining wine and cook for 5-10
minutes longer or until sausages are
cooked. Season with black pepper.

Serves 4

*Sausages with Onions and Wine, Fennel
Pea Purée, Beef Bourguignon*

LAMB WITH ROASTED GARLIC SAUCE

Oven temperature
180°C, 350°F, Gas 4

While this recipe uses a lot of garlic you will find that roasted garlic has a subtle and sweet flavour.

1 head of garlic, cloves separated
and peeled
4 canned anchovy fillets, drained
olive oil
freshly ground black pepper
2 kg/4 lb leg of lamb, trimmed
of excess fat
1 onion, finely chopped
1 carrot, finely chopped
2 stalks celery, finely chopped
¹/₂ cup/125 mL/4 fl oz dry
white wine
1 cup/250 mL/8 fl oz chicken stock
2 tablespoons chopped fresh parsley

1   Place 4 cloves garlic, anchovy fillets, 1 teaspoon oil and black pepper to taste in a food processor or blender and process to make a smooth paste.

2   Using a sharp knife make several slits in the lamb. Push a little paste into each slit, then rub remaining paste over surface of lamb. Set aside to marinate for 20-30 minutes or in the refrigerator overnight.

3   Drain lamb, reserving marinade and place in a baking dish. Add onion, carrot, celery, wine and remaining garlic to frying pan and cook, stirring, for 5 minutes.

4   Pour wine mixture into baking dish and bake, adding more wine to keep vegetables moist if necessary, for 1¹/₂-2 hours or until lamb is cooked to your liking. Transfer lamb to a large serving platter and set aside to keep warm.

5   Skim fat from cooking juices remaining in baking dish. Place juices with vegetables and garlic in a food processor or blender and process until smooth. Transfer mixture to a small saucepan, stir in stock and bring to the boil over a medium heat, reduce heat and simmer for 5 minutes or until sauce reduces and thickens and coats the back of a spoon. Stir in parsley and season to taste with black pepper. To serve, carve lamb and accompany with sauce.

Serves 6

Lamb with Roasted Garlic Sauce

Blanquette of Veal or Lamb

1 kg/2 lb diced veal or lean lamb
bouquet garni
1 onion, finely chopped
1 carrot, finely chopped
2 stalks celery, finely chopped
4 cups/1 litre/1³/₄ pt cold chicken stock
6 pickling onions or shallots
6 small carrots, scrubbed
12 small new potatoes
1 tablespoon olive oil
250 g/8 oz button mushrooms
¹/₂ cup/125 mL/4 fl oz dry white wine
2 teaspoons cornflour blended with
¹/₄ cup/60 mL/2 fl oz cream (single)
125 g/4 oz frozen petit pois (small peas)
2 tablespoons lemon juice
2 tablespoons low-fat natural yogurt
3 tablespoons chopped fresh parsley
freshly ground black pepper

5 Return stock to a clean pan, bring to the boil and boil for 15 minutes or until reduced to 1 cup/250 mL/8 fl oz of stock. Stir a little stock into cornflour mixture, then stir cornflour mixture into stock in pan. Bring to the boil and cook, stirring, until mixture thickens slightly.

6 Add reserved mushroom mixture, meat and vegetables to sauce, bring back to simmering, add peas and cook, stirring occasionally, for 5 minutes or until peas are cooked. Stir in lemon juice, yogurt, parsley and black pepper to taste and bring back to simmering.

Serves 6

A traditional blanquette is enriched with egg yolks and cream. In this version the egg yolks are omitted and replaced with yogurt and the cream is greatly reduced to give a dish that is just as tasty as the original, but much lighter in kilojoules (calories).

1 Bring a saucepan of water to the boil. Add meat, bring back to the boil and boil for 2 minutes. Drain meat, rinse under cold running water and drain again.

2 Place meat, bouquet garni, chopped onion, carrot, celery and stock in a clean saucepan and bring to the boil. Reduce heat and simmer for 45 minutes. Add pickling onions or shallots, carrots and potatoes and cook for 20 minutes longer or until meat and vegetables are tender.

3 Heat oil in a nonstick frying pan, add mushrooms and cook, stirring, for 5 minutes. Add wine, bring to simmering, cover and simmer for 5 minutes. Remove lid from pan, and simmer for 5 minutes or until juices are reduced by half. Remove pan from heat and set aside.

4 Using a slotted spoon remove meat and whole vegetables from stock mixture. Strain stock and discard bouquet garni and chopped vegetables.

Making Blanquette of Veal

Saucepan Accoutrement

43

Olive and Meat Ragout

1 tablespoon olive oil
500 g/1 lb chuck steak, trimmed of
all visible fat and cut into 2.5 cm/
1 in pieces
500 g/1 lb leg lamb, trimmed of
all visible fat and cut into 2.5 cm/
1 in pieces
3 onions, chopped
2 cloves garlic, crushed
1 teaspoon finely chopped fresh thyme
or $1/2$ teaspoon dried thyme
$1/2$ cup/125 mL/4 fl oz dry white wine
1 cup/250 mL/8 fl oz beef stock
440 g/14 oz canned tomatoes, undrained
and mashed
5 cm/2 in piece orange rind
bouquet garni
90 g/3 oz pitted black olives
2 tablespoons finely chopped fresh
parsley
freshly ground black pepper

1   Heat oil in a large saucepan over a medium heat, add beef and lamb and cook in batches until brown. Remove meat from pan and drain on absorbent kitchen paper.

2   Add onions, garlic and thyme to pan and cook, stirring, for 5 minutes or until onions are tender and golden. Return meat to pan, stir in wine, stock, tomatoes, orange rind and bouquet garni and bring to the boil. Reduce heat, cover and simmer for $1^1/2$ hours or until meat is tender. Discard orange rind and bouquet garni.

3   Using a slotted spoon remove meat from pan and set aside. Bring sauce remaining in pan to the boil and boil until it reduces and thickens. Return meat to pan, add olives, parsley and black pepper to taste and cook for 20 minutes.

Serves 6

As with most ragoûts or stews and casseroles this one will improve if made the day before then reheated just prior to serving.

Roast Pork with Fennel

1.5 kg/3 lb boneless pork loin
1 fennel bulb, thinly sliced
1 teaspoon fennel seeds
2 teaspoon fresh sage or 1 teaspoon
dried sage
freshly ground black pepper
1 cup/250 mL/8 fl oz dry white wine
2 tablespoons chopped fresh fennel
leaves

1   Unroll loin and make a cut in the middle of the fleshy part of the meat and lay out. Score rind at 2 cm/$^3/_4$ in intervals. Place pork, rind side down and top with a layer of fennel slices, leaving a 2 cm/$^3/_4$ in border. Sprinkle with half the fennel seeds and sage. Season with black pepper. Roll loin and tie with string. Place in a glass or ceramic dish, pour over wine, cover and

marinate in the refrigerator overnight.

2   Remove pork from wine mixture and place on a wire rack set in a flameproof baking dish. Reserve wine mixture. Sprinkle pork with remaining fennel seeds and sage and bake for 1 hour or until tender. Remove and set aside.

3   Pour reserved wine mixture into baking dish and bring to the boil over a high heat, stirring and scraping base of dish, for 2-3 minutes or until mixture reduces slightly. Slice pork, spoon over sauce and sprinkle with fennel leaves.

Serves 8

Roast Pork with Fennel, Olive and Meat Ragoût

When scoring pork rind take care not to cut too deeply. The cut should only be about 5 mm/$^1/_4$ in deep. Scoring makes the rind easier to cut when it is cooked.

Plates Accoutrement

MEATLESS MEALS

Vegetable dishes are an important part of French cooking. In southern France they are often the main dish while in other areas they enhance or complement a meat, fish, poultry or game dish. The recipes in this chapter are ideal for vegetarian meals and many make imaginative first courses.

LEEK TERRINE WITH ORANGE SAUCE

8 spinach or silverbeet leaves
10 leeks
2 large red peppers, seeded, quartered, roasted and skins removed
1 large yellow or green pepper, seeded, quartered, roasted and skins removed
freshly ground black pepper

MINTED ORANGE SAUCE
1¼ cup/250 g/8 oz low-fat natural yogurt
2 tablespoons finely grated orange rind
2 tablespoons finely chopped fresh mint

1   Line a 14 x 21 cm/5½ x 8½ in loaf tin with aluminium foil. Set aside.

2   Boil, steam or microwave spinach or silverbeet leaves until just wilted. Drain well. Line prepared loaf tin with overlapping spinach leaves. Allow leaves to overhang the sides of the tin by about 5 cm/2 in.

3   Boil or microwave leeks until soft. Drain, cut in half lengthwise and set aside.

4   Place a layer of leeks in the base of prepared loaf tin, then top with a layer of peppers and season to taste with black pepper. Repeat layers to use all ingredients and to fill tin. Fold overhanging spinach or silverbeet leaves over filling and cover with aluminium foil. Place a heavy weight on terrine and refrigerate overnight.

5   To make sauce, place yogurt, orange rind, mint and black pepper to taste in a bowl and mix to combine. To serve, unmould terrine, cut into slices and serve with sauce.

Serves 6

A colouful terrine that makes a wonderful lunch dish. Serve with crusty bread and a glass of dry white wine for a complete meal.

Leek Terrine with Orange Sauce

Plate Country Road

Aubergine Mousse

Oven temperature
180°C, 350°F, Gas 4

3 medium eggplant (aubergines)
1 tablespoon olive oil
3 spring onions, chopped
3 eggs, separated
$^1/_4$ cup/60 mL/2 fl oz cream (double)
1 teaspoon chopped fresh basil
freshly ground black pepper

Serve this mousse with Melba toast. To make Melba toast, cut bread into slices of a medium thickness and lightly toast. Cut crusts from toast and split each slice horizontally. Cut each slice in half diagonally and bake at 180°C/350°F/Gas 4 for 5-7 minutes or until the edges curl and the toast is golden.

1   Brush eggplant (aubergines) with oil, place on a baking tray and bake for 1 hour or until soft. Remove eggplant (aubergines) from oven and set aside until cool enough to handle. Cut eggplant (aubergines) in half and scoop out flesh.

2   Place eggplant (aubergine) flesh, spring onions, egg yolks, cream, basil and black pepper to taste in a food processor or blender and process until smooth. Transfer mixture to a bowl and set aside.

3   Place egg whites in a separate bowl and beat until stiff peaks form. Fold egg white mixture into eggplant (aubergine) mixture and spoon into a greased 20 cm/8 in round dish. Bake for 30 minutes or until set. Serve hot, warm or cold.

Serves 4

Asparagus Tarts

Oven temperature
180°C, 350°F, Gas 4

1 quantity Basic Pastry (page 72)
ASPARAGUS FILLING
30 g/1 oz butter
1 clove garlic, crushed
1 onion, finely chopped
250 g/8 oz asparagus, cut into 4 cm/
$1^1/_2$ in pieces
3 eggs, lightly beaten
$^1/_2$ cup/125 mL/4 fl oz cream (double)
3 tablespoons grated Parmesan cheese

This recipe can also be made as a 25 cm/10 in flan. Use a 25 cm/10 in flan tin with a removable base and increase the cooking time by 5-10 minutes.

1   To make filling, melt butter in a frying pan over a medium heat, add garlic and onion and cook, stirring, for 3 minutes or until onion is golden.

2   Add asparagus to pan and cook, stirring, for 5 minutes or until asparagus is bright green. Remove pan from heat and set aside to cool slightly.

3   Place eggs, cream and Parmesan cheese in a bowl and whisk to combine. Mix in asparagus mixture.

4   Prepare pastry as described in recipe. Divide pastry into six portions. Roll out each portion to 5 mm/$^1/_4$ in thick and large enough to line a 10 cm/4 in flan tin. Rest pastry for 10 minutes, then line tins and chill for 10 minutes. Line pastry cases with nonstick baking paper, fill with uncooked rice and bake for 10 minutes. Remove rice and paper and bake for 5 minutes longer or until pastry is golden. Set aside to cool.

5   Divide filling between pastry cases and bake for 15 minutes or until filling is set.

Serves 6

Asparagus Tarts, Aubergine Mousse

CHEESE SOUFFLE

Oven temperature
200°C, 400°F, Gas 6

30 g/1 oz Parmesan cheese
60 g/2 oz butter
$^{1}/_{3}$ cup/45 g/1$^{1}/_{2}$ oz flour
1$^{1}/_{2}$ cups/375 mL/12 fl oz reduced-fat
milk
6 egg yolks
125 g/4 oz Gruyère cheese
freshly ground black pepper
8 egg whites

1 Lightly grease four 1 cup/250 mL/
8 fl oz capacity soufflé dishes and sprinkle
with Parmesan cheese. Set aside.

2 Melt butter in a saucepan over a
medium heat, add flour and cook, stirring,
for 1 minute. Remove pan from heat and
gradually whisk in milk. Return pan to
heat and cook, stirring constantly, for 5
minutes or until sauce boils and thickens.
Remove pan from heat and whisk in egg
yolks, one at a time. Stir in Gruyère
cheese and black pepper to taste.

3 Place egg whites in a bowl and beat
until soft peaks form. Fold egg white
mixture into sauce, spoon mixture into
prepared soufflé dishes and bake for 20
minutes or until soufflés are puffed and
golden.

For the best volume have
egg whites at room
temperature before beating.
Egg whites for a soufflé
should be beaten until they
are stiff, but not dry. The bowl
that the egg whites are
beaten in must be clean and
grease free or they will not
beat up.

Serves 4

STUFFED ARTICHOKES

6 large globe artichokes
3 tablespoons lemon juice
30 g/1 oz butter
1 clove garlic, crushed
3 spring onions, chopped
155 g/5 oz mushrooms, sliced
1 tablespoon chopped fresh thyme or
1 teaspoon dried thyme
1¼ cup/250 g/8 oz low-fat
natural yogurt
1 cup/60 g/2 oz wholemeal
breadcrumbs, made from stale bread
60 g/2 oz grated Parmesan cheese
½ cup/125 mL/4 fl oz white wine
1 cup/250 mL/8 fl oz vegetable stock

Oven temperature
200°C, 400°F, Gas 6

1 Remove stems from artichokes. Cut off pointed end of each leaf and brush cut surfaces of artichokes with lemon juice. Place artichokes in a large bowl of cold water and set aside to soak for 10 minutes. Remove artichokes from water and using a teaspoon scoop out centres and scrape away any fibres lining the heart.

2 Melt butter in a frying pan over a medium heat, add garlic and spring onions and cook for 3 minutes. Add mushrooms and thyme and cook for 5 minutes longer or until mushrooms are soft. Remove pan from heat, drain off any liquid and set aside to cool slightly.

3 Fold yogurt into mushroom mixture. Spoon some of the mushroom mixture into the centre of each artichoke. Spoon remaining mixture between leaves of artichokes.

4 Place breadcrumbs and Parmesan cheese in a bowl and mix to combine. Sprinkle breadcrumb mixture over artichokes and place on a wire rack set in a baking dish. Pour wine and stock into dish and bake for 30 minutes or until artichokes are tender.

Serves 6

Catherine de Medici was fond of artichokes and it was she who introduced them to the French and encouraged their cultivation.

Left: Cheese Soufflé
Right: Stuffed Artichokes

Plate Villeroy & Boch

CHEESE-FILLED PEPPERS

Oven temperature
200°C, 400°F, Gas 6

2 large red peppers
2 large green peppers
315 g/10 oz ricotta or curd cheese,
drained
2 spring onions, chopped
1 tablespoon finely grated orange rind
2 tablespoons slivered almonds, toasted
2 tablespooons snipped fresh chives
$\frac{1}{2}$ cup/30 g/1 oz breadcrumbs, made
from stale bread
60 g/2 oz grated Parmesan cheese
freshly ground black pepper
2 egg whites

Serves 4

1   Cut red and green peppers in half lengthwise, remove seeds and membrane and place in a lightly greased baking dish.

2   Combine ricotta or curd cheese, spring onions, orange rind, almonds, chives, breadcrumbs, half the Parmesan cheese and black pepper to taste in a bowl.

3   Place egg whites in a bowl and beat until stiff peaks form. Fold egg white mixture into ricotta mixture and spoon into pepper halves. Sprinkle with remaining Parmesan cheese and bake for 15 minutes or until puffed and golden.

SUMMER VEGETABLE PIE

Oven temperature
190°C, 375°F, Gas 5

1 quantity Basic Pastry (page 72)
2 tablespoons olive oil
2 onions, thinly sliced
4 tomatoes, cut into thick slices
4 zucchini (courgettes), sliced
2 teaspoons chopped fresh thyme or
1 teaspoon dried thyme
freshly ground black pepper
2 tablespoons finely chopped fresh basil
2 tablespoons finely chopped fresh
parsley

1   Prepare pastry as described in recipe. Roll out to 5 mm/$\frac{1}{4}$ in thick and large enough to line a 25 cm/10 in flan tin with a removable base. Allow pastry to rest for 10 minutes before placing in tin. Line tin with pastry and chill for 10 minutes. Line pastry case with nonstick baking paper, fill with uncooked rice and bake for 15 minutes. Remove rice and paper and bake for 5 minutes longer or until pastry is golden. Set aside to cool.

2   Heat 1 tablespoon oil in a nonstick frying pan over a medium heat, add onions and cook, stirring frequently, for 5 minutes or until onions are soft. Using a slotted spoon remove from pan and cool. Add tomato slices to pan and cook for 5 minutes. Remove from pan and cool. Drain any juices from pan.

3   Heat remaining oil in pan, add zucchini (courgette) slices and cook for 5 minutes or until soft. Remove from pan and cool.

4   Scatter onion over base of pastry case, sprinkle with thyme and black pepper to taste. Arrange tomato slices and zucchini (courgette) slices, attractively, on top of onions, sprinkle with basil and parsley and black pepper to taste and bake for 15 minutes.

Serves 6-8

Summer Vegetable Pie, Cheese-filled Peppers

Serve this pie warm with a tossed green salad, crusty bread and a glass of dry white wine.

Plates Villeroy & Boch

SIDE DISHES

This exciting selection of recipes for side dishes will complement any main meal. Potato and Cheese Pancake is delicious served with ragoûts and roasts while Glazed Vegetables go with nearly every main meal.

RATATOUILLE

2 eggplant (aubergines), cut into
1 cm/¹/₂ in thick slices
salt
1 tablespoon olive oil
2 cloves garlic, crushed
1 large onion, cut into wedges
1 large red pepper, chopped
1 large green pepper, chopped
3 zucchini (courgettes), sliced
440 g/14 oz canned tomatoes, undrained
and mashed
90 g/3 oz black olives
freshly ground black pepper

1   Place eggplant (aubergines) slices in a colander set over a bowl and sprinkle with salt. Set aside to stand for 10 minutes, then rinse under cold running water and pat dry with absorbent kitchen paper.

2   Heat oil in a nonstick frying pan over a medium heat. Add garlic and onion and cook, stirring, for 3 minutes or until onion is golden.

3   Add eggplant (aubergine) slices to pan and cook, a few at a time for 5 minutes each side or until brown. Return eggplant (aubergines) to pan, add red pepper, green pepper, zucchini (courgettes), tomatoes and olives and bring to the boil. Reduce heat and simmer for 20 minutes or until mixture reduces and thickens. Season to taste with black pepper.

Serves 4

Ratatouille is a versatile dish that can be served as an accompaniment to a meal, as a first course or as a light meal with crusty bread. Serve it hot, warm or cold and if you make it in advance and reheat it, it tastes even better.

Ratatouille, Braised Artichokes and Beans

FENNEL PEA PUREE

3 tablespoons olive oil
2 cloves garlic, crushed
1 kg/2 lb fennel, sliced
250 g/8 oz frozen peas
1 cup/250 mL/8 fl oz vegetable stock
1 tablespoon chopped fresh mint
freshly ground black pepper

1   Heat oil in a large frying pan over a medium heat, add garlic and fennel and cook for 10 minutes or until fennel is soft.

2   Add peas, stock and mint and bring to the boil. Reduce heat and simmer for 5 minutes or until peas are cooked.

3   Place fennel mixture in batches in a food processor or blender and process until smooth. Place purée in a clean saucepan and cook over a low heat for 4-5 minutes or until heated through. Season to taste with black pepper.

Serves 6

Vegetable purées are very popular in French cuisine and almost any vegetable can be made into a purée. If you have a Mouli food mill use this rather than a food processor to make purées, as it gives a better texture.

BRAISED ARTICHOKES AND BEANS

30 g/1 oz butter
2 cloves garlic, crushed
2 onions, sliced
2 carrots, sliced
250 g/8 oz fresh broad beans, shelled or
125 g/4 oz frozen broad beans
440 g/14 oz canned artichoke hearts,
drained
1 cup/250 mL/8 fl oz vegetable stock
freshly ground black pepper

1   Melt butter in a frying pan over a medium heat, add garlic and onions and cook, stirring, for 3 minutes or until onions are soft.

2   Add carrots, beans, artichokes and stock and bring to the boil. Reduce heat and simmer for 10 minutes or until vegetables are tender. Season to taste with black pepper.

Serves 6

Broad beans also known as fava beans are one of the oldest cultivated vegetables in the Western world and have played a major role in the cuisine of the Mediterranean for centuries.

Dishes Accoutrement

Potato Gratin

POTATO GRATIN

1 kg/2 lb potatoes, thinly sliced
2 large onions, thinly sliced
2 tablespoons snipped fresh chives
freshly ground black pepper
1¼ cup/250 g/8 oz low-fat natural
yogurt
1 cup/250 mL/8 fl oz cream (double)
60 g/2 oz grated Parmesan cheese

1 Layer potatoes, onions, chives and black pepper to taste in six lightly greased individual ovenproof dishes.

2 Place yogurt and cream in a bowl and mix to combine. Carefully pour yogurt mixture over potatoes and sprinkle with Parmesan cheese. Bake for 45 minutes or until potatoes are tender and top is golden.

Serves 6

Oven temperature
200°C, 400°F, Gas 6

Potato dishes such as this one are great accompaniments to almost any main meal. This one is particularly good served with Roast Pork with Fennel (page 44) or Lamb with Roasted Garlic Sauce (page 42).

GLAZED VEGETABLES

12 small carrots, scrubbed
12 small turnips, scrubbed
12 pickling onions or shallots
12 small new potatoes, scrubbed
1 tablespoon honey
2 tablespoons olive oil

1   Place carrots, turnips, onions and potatoes in a lightly greased baking dish.

2   Place honey and oil in a small bowl and mix to combine. Brush vegetables with honey mixture and bake, basting frequently, for 30 minutes or until vegetables are cooked.

Serves 6

Oven temperature
200°C, 400°F, Gas 6

Other vegetables you might like to cook in this way are small zucchini (courgettes), eggplant (aubergines) and parsnips. Zucchini (courgettes) will only take about 15 minutes to cook.

BEANS IN RICH TOMATO SAUCE

500 g/1 lb dried lima beans
1 tablespoon olive oil
1 clove garlic, crushed
1 onion, finely chopped
3 tablespoons chopped fresh parsley
1 tablespoon chopped fresh rosemary or
1 teaspoon dried rosemary
440 g/14 oz canned tomatoes, undrained and mashed
freshly ground black pepper

1   Place beans in a large bowl, cover with water and set aside to soak overnight.

2   Drain beans, place in a saucepan with enough water to cover and bring to the boil. Boil for 10 minutes, then reduce heat and simmer for 1 hour or until tender. Drain and set aside.

3   Heat oil in a large saucepan, add garlic and onion and cook, stirring, for 3 minutes or until onion is golden. Add parsley, rosemary and tomatoes and bring to the boil. Reduce heat and simmer, stirring occasionally, for 20 minutes or until mixture reduces and thickens. Stir in beans and black pepper to taste and cook for 15 minutes longer.

Serves 6

This dish also makes a good vegetarian main meal. If serving as a main meal this recipe will serve 4, for a complete meal accompany with crusty bread and a tossed green salad.

Beans in Rich Tomato Sauce

WILD RICE PILAU

30 g/1 oz butter
1 clove garlic, crushed
1 onion, finely chopped
3 spring onions, chopped
200 g/6$^1/_2$ oz wild rice or a mix of brown and wild rices
2 cups/500 mL/16 fl oz chicken stock
1 tablespoon chopped fresh sage or 1 teaspoon dried sage
1 tablespoon chopped fresh rosemary or 1 teaspoon dried rosemary

1   Melt butter in a large saucepan over a medium heat, add garlic, onion and spring onions and cook for 3 minutes or until onion is golden.

2   Add rice and cook, stirring, for 5 minutes. Add stock, sage and rosemary and bring to the boil. Reduce heat and simmer, adding more stock if necessary, for 45-60 minutes or until rice is tender.

Serves 4-6

Wild rice while not traditionally used in French cooking is just as popular there now as it is elsewhere in the world.

POTATO AND CHEESE PANCAKE

1 kg/2 lb potatoes, grated
2 eggs, lightly beaten
2 onions, grated
2 tablespoons flour
1 teaspoon finely chopped fresh
coriander
60 g/2 oz reduced-fat Cheddar cheese,
grated
freshly ground black pepper
2 tablespoons olive oil
6 tablespoons low-fat natural yogurt

1 Rinse potatoes in a colander under cold running water, then turn onto a clean teatowel or absorbent kitchen paper and pat dry.

2 Place potatoes, eggs, onions, flour, coriander, Cheddar cheese and black pepper to taste in a bowl and mix to combine.

3 Heat oil in a large nonstick frying pan over a medium heat, spread potato mixture over base of pan and cook for 15 minutes. Place pan under a preheated medium grill and cook for 10 minutes or until top is golden and pancake is cooked through. Serve cut into wedges and topped with yogurt.

A delicious accompaniment to meat and fish dishes this pancake is equally as good served with a tossed green salad for a light meal.

Serves 6-8

Plates Accoutrement

Plate Country Road

Left: Potato and Cheese Pancake
Above: Dijon Mushrooms

DIJON MUSHROOMS

30 g/1 oz butter
4 pickling onions or shallots,
finely chopped
1 clove garlic, crushed
500 g/1 lb mushrooms
3/4 cup/185 mL/6 fl oz dry white wine
1 tablespoon Dijon mustard
1 teaspoon finely chopped fresh
coriander
1¼ cup/250 g/8 oz low-fat
natural yogurt
freshly ground black pepper
2 tablespoons chopped fresh parsley

Serves 6

1 Melt butter in a nonstick frying pan over a medium heat, add onions or shallots and garlic and cook, stirring, for 2-3 minutes or until onions or shallots are soft.

2 Add mushrooms and cook, stirring occasionally, for 5 minutes or until mushrooms are cooked. Remove mushrooms from pan, set aside and keep warm.

3 Stir wine, mustard and coriander into pan and bring to the boil. Reduce heat and simmer for 10 minutes or until liquid reduces by half. Remove pan from heat stir in yogurt and season to taste with black pepper. Return pan to a low heat and cook for 2-3 minutes or until heated through. Spoon sauce over mushrooms, sprinkle with parsley and serve.

A great accompaniment to a roast or serve with Melba toast for an elegant starter. To make Melba toast see hint on page 48.

61

PERFECT FINISHES

Many of the best French desserts are fruit based. Here you will find a selection of light desserts that won't ruin your diet.

FRENCH APPLE TART

Oven temperature
190°C, 375°F, Gas 5

1 quantity Basic Pastry (page 72)
2 green apples, peeled and cored
1 tablespoon lemon juice
1 tablespoon caster sugar

APPLE FILLING
750 g/1¹/₂ lb green apples, peeled, cored
and chopped
1 cup/250 mL/8 fl oz water
2 tablespoons caster sugar
30 g/1 oz butter
¹/₂ teaspoon ground cinnamon
¹/₂ teaspoon ground nutmeg
1 tablespoon lemon juice
1 teaspoon finely grated lemon rind
1 tablespoon brandy

APRICOT GLAZE
3 tablespoons apricot jam, sieved

1   To make filling, place chopped apples and water in a heavy-based saucepan, cover and cook over a medium heat, stirring frequently, until apples are very soft. Turn into a sieve set over a bowl and drain for 10 minutes. Reserve juices.

2   Place cooked apples, caster sugar, butter, cinnamon, nutmeg, lemon juice, lemon rind and brandy in a food processor or blender and process to make a purée.

Cook purée over a low heat, stirring frequently, until a thick paste forms. Set aside to cool completely.

3   Make pastry as described in recipe. Roll out pastry to 5 mm/¹/₄ in thick and large enough to line a 23 cm/9 in flan tin. Rest pastry for 10 minutes, then line tin and chill for 10 minutes. Line pastry case with nonstick baking paper, fill with uncooked rice and bake for 15 minutes. Remove rice and paper and bake for 5 minutes longer. Set aside to cool.

4   Cut remaining apples into neat slices and toss in lemon juice. Spread purée over base of pastry case. Arrange apple slices overlapping on top of purée, sprinkle with caster sugar and bake for 25-30 minutes or until apples are tender.

5   To make glaze, cook apricot jam and 1 tablespoon reserved apple juice in a small saucepan over a low heat, stirring, for 5 minutes or until a thick syrupy glaze forms. Brush hot glaze over hot tart and set aside to cool. Serve warm or cold.

Serves 8

The easiest way to cut apples into neat slices is to first cut the apples into quarters then to slice it.
Serve this tart with natural yogurt flavoured with honey and ground nutmeg.

French Apple Tart

Plates, cup and saucer Villeroy & Boch

Raspberry Mousse

500 g/1 lb fresh or frozen raspberries
2 teaspoons gelatine dissolved in
2 tablespoons hot water, cooled
125 g/4 oz ricotta or curd cheese,
drained
4 eggs, separated
$^{1}/_{4}$ cup/60 g/2 oz caster sugar
whipped cream
chocolate curls, to garnish (optional)

To make chocolate curls, using a vegetable peeler, shave the sides of a block of chocolate. For curls to form the chocolate should be at room temperature. If the chocolate is chilled shavings will form.

1 Place raspberries in a food processor or blender and process to make a purée. Push purée through a sieve to remove seeds and set aside. Stir gelatine mixture into purée and set aside.

2 Place ricotta or curd cheese in a food processor or blender and process until smooth. Set aside.

3 Place egg yolks and sugar in a heatproof bowl, set over a saucepan of simmering water and beat until a ribbon trail forms when beater is lifted from mixture. Remove bowl from heat. Whisk egg yolk mixture, then ricotta or curd cheese into raspberry purée. Cover and chill until just beginning to set.

4 Place egg whites in a bowl and beat until stiff peaks form. Fold egg white mixture into fruit mixture. Spoon mousse mixture into four lightly oiled $^{1}/_{2}$ cup/ 125 mL/4 fl oz capacity moulds or ramekins, cover and chill until set.

5 To serve, garnish with chocolate curls.

Serves 4

CHOCOLATE SOUFFLE

$^1/_4$ cup/30 g/1 oz cornflour
30 g/1 oz ground almonds
$^3/_4$ cup/185 mL/6 fl oz milk
1 tablespoon strong black coffee
75 g/2$^1/_2$ oz dark chocolate, broken
into pieces
2 teaspoons caster sugar
2 eggs yolks
1 tablespoon coffee-flavoured liqueur
4 egg whites
1 tablespoon brown sugar
1 tablespoon icing sugar, sifted

1   Sift cornflour and almonds together into a bowl and make a well in the centre. Set aside.

2   Place milk and coffee in saucepan and bring to the boil over a medium heat. Slowly whisk milk mixture into almond mixture and continue whisking until smooth. Return mixture to saucepan and bring to the boil over a medium heat, stirring constantly. As soon as the mixture comes to the boil, remove pan from heat.

3   Stir chocolate and caster sugar into milk mixture and continue stirring until chocolate melts. Whisk egg yolks and liqueur into milk mixture, cover and set aside to keep warm.

4   Place egg whites in a bowl and beat until soft peaks form. Gradually beat in brown sugar and continue beating until stiff peaks form. Whisk one-third of the egg white mixture into the chocolate mixture, then fold in remaining egg white mixture.

5   Pour soufflé mixture into a greased 20 cm/8 in soufflé dish and bake for 20 minutes or until well risen. Sprinkle with icing sugar and serve immediately.

Serves 6

Oven temperature
180°C, 350°F, Gas 4

Egg whites at room temperature beat up more rapidly and have a better volume than those straight out of the refrigerator. Correctly beaten egg whites will increase by 7-8 times their original volume.

Left: Raspberry Mousse
Right: Chocolate Soufflé

65

APRICOT LIQUEUR SOUFFLE

Oven temperature
180°C, 350°F, Gas 4

To test if a soufflé is cooked, shake the dish gently. If the soufflé wobbles all over, cook for 5 minutes longer. Always serve a soufflé immediately it is cooked, as it deflates shortly after being removed from the oven.

8 canned apricot halves in natural juice,
well drained
1 tablespoon orange liqueur
1 tablespoon caster sugar
4 egg whites
1 tablespoon icing sugar, sifted

Serves 4

1   Place apricots, liqueur and 2 teaspoons caster sugar in a food processor or blender and process to make a purée. Place purée in a small saucepan and cook, stirring, over a low heat for 2-3 minutes or until mixture thickens and some of the moisture evaporates. Remove pan from heat and set aside.

2   Place egg whites in a bowl and beat until soft peaks form, add remaining caster sugar and beat until stiff peaks form. Fold egg white mixture into apricot purée. Spoon mixture into four lightly greased $^1/_2$ cup/125 mL/4 fl oz capacity soufflé dishes and bake for 12-15 minutes or until soufflés are puffed and golden. Dust with icing sugar and serve immediately.

FRENCH MADELEINES

Oven temperature
200°C, 400°F, Gas 6

Madeleine tins are available from speciality cookware shops. They come in a sheet (like patty cake tins) and have elongated shell-shaped depressions.
Madeleines are delicious served with desserts such as Raspberry Mousse or as an afternoon treat. They will keep in an airtight container for up to a week and also freeze well.

2 eggs
$^1/_4$ cup/60 g/2 oz caster sugar
1 teaspoon orange flower water
(optional)
$^1/_2$ cup/60 g/2 oz flour, sifted
60 g/2 oz butter, melted and cooled

1   Place eggs and sugar in a heatproof bowl set over a saucepan of simmering water and beat until a ribbon trail forms when beater is lifted from mixture. Remove bowl from heat, beat in orange flower water (if using) and continue beating for 2 minutes longer.

2   Sift flour over egg mixture and fold in. Fold butter into batter and divide mixture between twelve greased and floured madeleine tins. Bake for 10-12 minutes or until Madeleines are cooked and golden. Stand in tins for 1 minute before turning onto a wire rack to cool.

Makes 12

Apricot Liqueur Soufflé, French Madeleines

CREPES SUZETTE

½ cup/125 mL/4 fl oz orange juice, warmed
2 tablespoons caster sugar
1 tablespoon orange-flavoured liqueur
1 tablespoon brandy

CREPES
1 cup/125 g/4 oz flour
¾ cup/185 mL/6 fl oz reduced-fat milk
½ cup/125 mL/4 fl oz water
2 eggs
15 g/½ oz butter, melted
1 tablespoon sugar

To keep cooked crêpes warm while making the rest of the batch, place the crêpes in a stack on a heatproof plate and place in a low oven, or over a saucepan of simmering water. Alcohol needs to be warmed to flambé effectively, however, take care not to overheat or it will evaporate before it you can ignite it.

1 To make crêpes, place flour, milk, water, eggs, butter and sugar in a food processor or blender and process until smooth. Cover and set aside to stand for 1 hour.

2 Pour 2-3 tablespoons batter into a heated, lightly greased 18 cm/7 in crêpe pan and tilt pan so batter covers base thinly and evenly. Cook over a high heat for 1 minute or until lightly browned. Turn crêpe and cook on second side for 30 seconds. Remove from pan, set aside and keep warm. Repeat with remaining batter to make twelve crêpes.

3 Fold crêpes into quarters and arrange overlapping in a heatproof dish. Pour over orange juice and sprinkle with caster sugar. Place orange liqueur and brandy in a small saucepan and warm over a low heat, ignite, pour over crêpes and serve immediately.

Serves 4

FRUIT BRULEE

500 g/1 lb rhubarb, trimmed and cut
into 5 cm/2 in pieces
$^1/_2$ cup/125 mL/4 fl oz water
$^1/_4$ cup/60 g/2 oz sugar
250 g/8 oz low-fat natural yogurt
3 eggs, lightly beaten
1 tablespoon almond liqueur (optional)
$^1/_4$ cup/45 g/1$^1/_2$ oz brown sugar

1   Place rhubarb, water and sugar in a
saucepan and cook over a medium heat
for 15-20 minutes or until rhubarb is
cooked and most of the liquid has
evaporated. Spread rhubarb over the base
of a lightly greased ovenproof dish and
set aside.

2   Place yogurt, eggs, liqueur (if using),
and 1 tablespoon brown sugar in bowl and
beat to combine. Pour yogurt mixture
over rhubarb mixture. Place dish in a
baking dish with enough boiling water to
come halfway up the sides of the dish and
bake for 30 minutes or until set.

3   Sift remaining brown sugar over top of
brûlée and cook under a preheated hot
grill for 2-3 minutes or until sugar just melts.

Serves 4

Left: Crêpes Suzette
Above: Fruit Brûlée

Oven temperature
160°C, 325°F, Gas 3

This dessert is delicious served
hot, warm or chilled.

PLUM CLAFOUTIS

Oven temperature
180°C, 350°F, Gas 4

Clafoutis can be made with
any fruit that you wish.
Apricots and cherries are also
popular choices.

500 g/1 lb dark plums, halved and
stoned, or 440 g/14 oz canned plums,
well drained
1 cup/125 g/4 oz self-raising flour
3 eggs
¹/₂ cup/100 g/3¹/₂ oz caster sugar
¹/₂ cup/125 mL/4 fl oz reduced-fat milk
1 tablespoon icing sugar, sifted

1   Arrange plums, cut side down, in a
lightly greased 25 cm/10 in flan dish.

2   Sift flour into a bowl and make a well
in the centre. Break eggs into well, add
caster sugar and milk and mix to form a
smooth batter.

3   Pour batter over plums and bake for
45 minutes or until firm and golden.
Serve hot, warm or cold, sprinkled with
icing sugar.

Serves 6

SNOW EGGS WITH ROSE CUSTARD

SNOW EGG MERINGUES
3 egg whites
1 tablespoon caster sugar
1 teaspoon lemon juice
1 cup/250 mL/8 fl oz reduced-fat milk

ROSE CUSTARD
3 egg yolks
2 tablespoons caster sugar
³/₄ cup/155 g/5 oz low-fat natural yogurt
1 teaspoon rose water
2 tablespoons raspberry purée

CRYSTALLIZED ROSE PETALS
12 pink or red rose petals
1 egg white, lightly beaten
2 tablespoons caster sugar

1 To make Crystallized Rose Petals, brush rose petals with egg white, sprinkle with sugar, place on nonstick baking paper and set aside in a warm place to dry.

2 To make meringues, place egg whites in a bowl and beat until soft peaks form. Continue beating while slowly adding sugar, then beat in lemon juice and beat until stiff peaks form.

3 Place milk in a large frying pan and bring to simmering over a medium heat. Using two tablespoons shape spoonfuls of egg white mixture and poach in milk for 2-3 minutes or until cooked. Using a slotted spoon remove meringues from milk and drain on absorbent kitchen paper. Reserve milk.

4 To make custard, place egg yolks and sugar in a heatproof bowl and whisk until thick and creamy. Continue beating while slowly pouring in reserved hot milk. Place bowl over a saucepan of simmering water and cook, stirring constantly, until mixture thickens and coats the back of a metal spoon. Remove bowl from pan and set aside to cool for 5 minutes. Stir yogurt, rose water and raspberry purée into custard mixture. Place bowl in iced water and stir until custard is cold.

5 To serve, divide custard between four dessert plates, top with three meringues and scatter with rose petals.

Serves 4

To make raspberry purée, place fresh or frozen raspberries in a food processor or blender and process to make a purée, push mixture through a sieve to remove seeds and use as desired.

Left: Plum Clafoutis
Right: Snow Eggs with Rose Custard

Fabric Redelman & Son

SECRETS TO SUCCESS

To capture the true essence of French cooking, homemade stocks are a must. In this chapter there are recipes for making your own wonderful stocks and a recipe for a reduced-fat pastry.

BASIC PASTRY

This dough must be rested after rolling out and chilled after placing in the tin and before cooking.

The fat content of the pastry has been decreased by one-quarter and omitting the egg will further decrease the kilojoule (calorie) content of the pastry. If omitting the egg, the pastry will not be as rich and you will need to add more water.

1 cup/155 g/5 oz wholemeal flour
³/₄ cup/90 g/3 oz flour
pinch salt
90 g/3 oz butter
1 egg (optional)
2-3 tablespoons iced water (extra will be required if the egg is omitted)

1   Place wholemeal flour, flour and salt in a food processor and process to combine. Add butter and process until mixture resembles fine breadcrumbs.

2   With machine running, add egg (if using) and enough water to form a rough dough. Turn dough onto a lightly floured surface and knead briefly. Wrap dough in plastic food wrap and refrigerate for 20 minutes. Use as desired.

BOUQUET GARNI

2 sprigs fresh parsley
2 sprigs fresh thyme
1 fresh or dried bay leaf

Place herb stems together and tie with string. Use as desired.

CHICKEN STOCK

1 chicken carcass, skin removed and
trimmed of all visible fat
1 onion, quartered
2 carrots, roughly chopped
4 stalks celery, roughly chopped
fresh herbs of your choice
$^1/_2$ teaspoon black peppercorns
3 litres/5 pt cold water

1   Place chicken carcass, onion, carrots,
celery, herbs, peppercorns and water in a
large saucepan. Bring to the boil over a
medium heat, reduce heat and simmer,
stirring occasionally, for 2 hours.

2   Strain stock and refrigerate overnight.

3   Skim fat from surface of stock and use
as required or freeze.

Makes 2 litres/3$^1/_2$ pt

BEEF STOCK

500 g/1 lb shin beef, diced
500 g/1 lb marrow bones, cut into pieces
1 onion, quartered
2 carrots, roughly chopped
4 stalks celery, roughly chopped
fresh herbs of your choice
4 peppercorns
3 litres/5 pt cold water

1   Place beef, bones, onion, carrots,
celery, herbs, peppercorns and water in a
large saucepan. Bring to the boil over a
medium heat, reduce heat and simmer,
stirring occasionally, for 2 hours.

2   Strain stock and refrigerate overnight.

3   Skim fat from surface of stock and use
as required or freeze.

Makes 2 litres/3$^1/_2$ pt

This recipe will make a rich
stock. The meat can be
omitted and only the bones
used if you wish.

FISH STOCK

Fish stock is even better if you can include the shells of lobster, prawns or crab. When making fish stock it is important that the cooking time is no longer than 20 minutes as the bones and trimmings become bitter and impart an unpleasant taste to the stock.

fish bones, skins and seafood shells, the quantity and type used is not important
1 large onion, quartered
1 large carrot, roughly chopped
4 stalks celery, roughly chopped
1 bay leaf
1 sprig fresh thyme
¹/₂ teaspoon black peppercorns
3 litres/5 pt cold water

1   Place fish bones and trimmings, onion, carrot, celery, bay leaf, thyme, peppercorns and water in a large saucepan. Bring to the boil over a medium heat, reduce heat and simmer for 20 minutes.

2   Strain stock and use as required or freeze.

Makes 2 litres/3¹/₂ pt

VEGETABLE STOCK

2 large onions, quartered
2 large carrots, roughly chopped
1 bunch celery, leaves included, roughly chopped
1 large bunch parsley, stalks included, roughly chopped
¹/₂ teaspoon black peppercorns
2.5 litres/4 pt cold water

1   Place onions, carrots, celery, parsley, peppercorns and water in a large saucepan. Bring to the boil over a medium heat, reduce heat and simmer, stirring occasionally, for 30 minutes.

2   Remove pan from heat and set aside to cool.

3   Purée cold vegetable mixture, then push through a sieve and use as required or freeze.

Makes 2 litres/3¹/₂ pt

The best vegetable stock ever – well worth the effort to make. It will add a delicious flavour to any soup or casserole and is a must for any vegetarian.

MENU IDEAS

Use these menu suggestions to create your own French style meals. Whether you a having a summer lunch or a winter dinner party from recipes in this book you will be able to present a truly delicious meal.

A SUMMER LUNCHEON
FOR EIGHT
Served buffet-style in the garden or on the patio this casual summer luncheon is an easy way to entertain friends.

**Mixed Vegetable Platter with
Tapenade**
(page 14)

Tomato Tart
(page 12)
Chicken and Fresh Herb Terrine
(page 8)
Summer Vegetable Pie
(page 52)
Crusty French Bread Sticks

French Apple Tart
(page 62)

French Madeleines
(page 66)
Coffee

FAMILY DINNER FOR SIX
Chicken Cassoulet
(page 26)
Tossed Green Salad

Fruit Brûlée
(page 69)

FIRESIDE SUPPER FOR FOUR
French Onion Soup
(page 6)
Warm Chickpea Salad
(page 12)
Crusty French Rolls

Plum Clafoutis
(page 70)

WINTER DINNER PARTY
FOR FOUR
Vegetable Soup with Pistou
(page 4)

Duck with Ratatouille
(page 30)
Wild Rice Pilau
(page 59)

Fruit Brûlée
(page 69)

VEGETARIAN DINNER
FOR FOUR
Garlic and Parsley Soup
(page 6)

Cheese Soufflé
(page 50)

Potato and Cheese Pancake
(page 60)
Tossed Green Salad

Crêpes Suzette
(page 68)

INDEX